BWB

D0969117

To Robert —
Hope this leads to a
" Kindness revolution" (p.64)
Best wishes
Ned Howell
9·27·95

MORE THAN WORDS

MORE
THAN
WORDS

Nine Silver Rules For
Powerful Yet Considerate
Communication

Edward Horrell

CENTER *for* SPOKEN
COMMUNICATION

Copyright ©1995 by Edward Horrell. Printed and bound in the United States of America. All rights reserved. No part of this book may be reproduced in any form or by any electronic or mechanical means including information storage and retrieval systems without permission in writing from the publisher, except by a reviewer, who may quote brief passages in a review. Published by Center for Spoken Communication, Inc., 1755 Kirby Parkway, Suite 240, Memphis, TN 38120-4392.

10   9   8   7   6   5   4   3   2   1

The following trademarks appear in this book: PEZ and Gerber's. These names are used in an editorial fashion only with no intention of infringement of the trademark.

Library of Congress Catalog Card Number: 94-74916

ISBN 0-9644788-0-3

Editing, book and book jacket design produced by Oden & Associates.

Attention Colleges and Universities, Corporations, and Professional Organizations: Quantity discounts are available on bulk purchases of this book for educational training purposes, fund raising, or gift giving. Special books, booklets, or book excerpts can also be created to fit your specific needs. For information contact:

Center for Spoken Communication, Inc.
1755 Kirby Parkway, Suite 240
Memphis, TN 38120-4392

Acknowledgments

In past and present roles as manager, parent, partner, son, spouse, friend, and public speaker, I have discovered one essential formula . . . people respond nicer to courtesy than to discourteous communication. People want to be treated with decency.

The purpose of my writing this book is to hopefully remind readers of the importance of treating people with respect.

The skills mentioned herein are those which are taught regularly in my seminars and workshops. I have observed the power of putting them into practice; I have witnessed the results of thousands of attendees who have testified to their successful use of these skills.

I do not claim authorship of some of these skills. Others are indeed of my own design. All are the result of studying and practicing techniques from various behavioral studies, books, tapes, workshops, and videos of numerous authors and presenters.

My role, then, is to serve as a messenger. It is my intent in writing this book to "tell the story" of how simple but powerful is the secret of putting kindness and thoughtfulness into our daily conversations at work and home.

There are many people whom I want to acknowledge for their help and support.

To my "literary agent," Kathy Tuberville of Oden & Associates, thank you for keeping me on track and focused.

To my editor, Rikki Boyce, thanks for helping me find the right words.

To my friend, confidant, and business partner Bill Plough, thanks for your unending support and enthusiasm for this project.

To my precious Mother, who up until her very last days always looked for the good in everybody she met, thanks for showing me that there is indeed something good in every person.

To my Dad, thanks for letting me observe how to live a life of dignity.

To Elaine, thanks for letting me observe how to command respect instead of demanding it.

To L. A., Wendy, and L. J., thanks for letting me observe firsthand how to be nice to people.

And finally, but most importantly, this book is dedicated to my best friends — my sons, Ted and Wilson. Thanks for being the best.

How to Contact the Author

Through the Center for Spoken Communication, Inc., the author provides seminars and consulting services for selected businesses, associations, and nonprofit organizations nationwide. Requests for information about these services, as well as inquiries about availability for speeches and seminars, should be directed to the address below. Readers of this book are also encouraged to contact the author with comments and ideas for future editions.

Edward Horrell
Center for Spoken Communication, Inc.
1755 Kirby Parkway, Suite 240
Memphis, TN 38120-4392
Or call:
901-755-9778

TABLE OF CONTENTS

Acknowledgments v

How to Contact the Author vi

Introduction viii

Silver Rule #1: The Rule of Difference 1

Silver Rule #2: The Rule of Agendas 15

Silver Rule #3: The Rule of Regard 25

Silver Rule #4: The Rule of Empathy 33

Silver Rule #5: The Rule of Listening 41

Silver Rule #6: The Rule of Respect 51

Silver Rule #7: The Rule of Signals 67

Silver Rule #8: The Rule of Dignity 75

Silver Rule #9: The Rule of Support 83

Communication on the Job 95

Communicating to Groups 101

Skill-Building Resources 111

Chart 1: Guide to Anticipated Behavior 112

Chart 2: How to Understand the Animals Better 113

Chart 3: A Checklist of Communication Skills: Self-Evaluation 114

Chart 4: A Checklist of Communication Skills: A Listener's Evaluation ...115

Chart 5: Group Presentation Checklist 116

Resources and Suggested Reading 117

Introduction

"I never get any respect."
— Rodney Dangerfield

Dignity and respect. Courtesy and kindness.

They are probably life's most essential ingredients. They are the attributes that motivate people to buy our products, work for our companies, spend time with us as friends.

People are crying out to be treated with dignity. To receive some respect for their feelings. To be treated with courtesy, thoughtfulness, and kindness. Our children, our customers, our friends, our employees, everyone longs for the same thing.

Show Some Dignity and Respect

In every instance of world-class communication, from one-on-one discussions to major public addresses, I have observed that effective speakers communicate more with their attitudes than with their words. And listeners who are treated with dignity and respect are always ready and willing to hear more.

There are specific ways we can convey these positive attitudes and treat people with courtesy. Unfortunately, there are also specific ways we convey a lack of dignity and respect for our listeners. And when our attitude doesn't convey the basic common courtesy of dignity and respect, even the most beautifully crafted, logical, and clever speech in the world will be wasted.

All too often, our attitudes send a different message to people we're talking to than our words do. Some of these attitudes can run counter to what we are trying to convey.

We don't convey dignity and respect . . .

. . . when we resent another person's style instead of appreciating, and even celebrating, the difference.

. . . when we fail to take the other person's agenda into consideration.

. . . when we fail to look the other person in the eye and call them by their name.

. . . when we don't empathize with the other person.

. . . when we fail to listen.

. . . when we don't show respect for the feelings of the other person.

. . . when we are unaware of the messages our nonverbal signals communicate.

. . . when we place a higher value on what someone does than how they do it.

. . . when we constantly poke holes in the other person's dreams and visions.

The problem for many of us is that we are unaware of when we're failing to convey dignity and respect to the people to whom we are speaking.

I believe it's time to stop and look at ourselves to see how we can become more effective by putting a little courtesy in our communication.

And that is why I have written this book.

Greek legend tells of an orator by the name of Demosthenes. Demosthenes was not an accomplished public speaker. He stuttered.

But Demosthenes overcame his stuttering to become one of the best-known speakers in history.

He put nuggets in his mouth, which corrected his stuttering.

My purpose here is to share some of the most successful "courtesy nuggets" I have accumulated over years of teaching communication skills. I know that as you practice these techniques, you'll discover for yourself how effective they are on a daily basis in every type of communication. Just like the numerous attendees of my workshops and seminars, you will find that people respond positively when they are being treated thoughtfully.

Common Sense Is Not Always Common

Recently, my partner and I were explaining our services and techniques to a senior official of a Fortune 100 company. After listening to us describe the importance of infusing communication with courtesy values, she said, "But, isn't this common sense stuff?"

It is.

But just as common sense tells us to eat a healthy diet, and not drive too fast, and to buckle our seat belts, we still need to be reminded.

My goal in writing this book is to introduce important values in the way we communicate. The values I'm talking about should come as no surprise at this point: treating other people with dignity, with respect, and with a celebration of our differences.

The Silver Rules

By following certain rules, we can convey these values in all our communication. This makes the messages we send much stronger than words alone.

We'll call them Silver Rules.

Of course, the Golden Rule is infallible, and comes first of all: Do unto others as you would have others do unto you.

But the Golden Rule does not work in communication.

We don't want to communicate to others the way we want to be communicated to . . . we want to communicate to others in the way they desire to be communicated with!

This is the essence of the Silver Rules of Communication.

The Silver Rules help us remember that everyone has different styles, different agendas, different ways of doing things. They're carrying around different "stuff" than us. As good communicators, we must learn to listen to their story, celebrate their different behavioral styles, and empathize.

Basically, the Silver Rules help us to do unto others as they would like us to do unto them, by communicating to others in the way they would like to be communicated with. Even though it differs from the way in which we might wish to be spoken to.

It is my goal, and the goal of everyone at the Center for Spoken Communication, to help people, companies, and families put some kindness and consideration into their interpersonal communication through the use of these Silver Rules.

And by adding these ingredients . . . kindness and consideration, dignity and respect . . . we will dramatically improve our personal and business communication. "Total Quality," the buzzword of business today, is impossible without considerate communication. And considerate communication is impossible without following the Silver Rules.

I have devoted a separate chapter to each of these important Silver Rules, with practical information on how to use them with clients, co-workers, bosses, employees, friends, and family.

Make it a point to focus on a new one every day, and soon you will discover that your interpersonal communication skills have improved, and that people are more comfortable with you.

And more willing to listen to what you have to say.

I have attempted to format the skills required for using the Silver Rules by placing "how-to" charts at the end of each chapter. It is my desire to "challenge" you to practice using these Rules in your daily communication with everyone.

But it will take some work. All important things do.

It is like the gift a young South African boy brought his teacher one Christmas: a shell from a beach the teacher knew was miles down the coast.

The boy beamed as his teacher admired the shell. "This is beautiful," exclaimed the teacher, "but you shouldn't have walked so far to get me a gift."

With a glowing smile, the boy replied, "The long walk is part of the gift!"

Courteous conversation requires some effort, some thought. For some of us, it is not easy.

But the effort . . . the long walk . . . is part of the gift.

And what better present could we give or receive than thoughtfulness in our communication?

It might just be the most treasured gift of all!

Before We Begin

"Insist on yourself; never imitate."
— *Ralph Waldo Emerson*

This book will explore the power we all have to convey feelings of dignity, respect, courtesy, and kindness to the people with whom we communicate.

It is about how we communicate with our attitudes. How we look at others. How we communicate our regard. Or disregard. Through our eyes, our bodies, our tone of voice, and our listening as well as the words we speak.

But before we begin, I would submit that these attitudes are difficult, if not impossible, to convey if we don't feel them for ourselves.

How can we convey dignity to others if we have no sense of dignity for ourselves and what we do?

How can we convey respect for others if we don't respect ourselves?

How can we support the dreams and visions of others if we don't have our own?

It begins with feeling good about ourselves!

It begins with having feelings of dignity and respect for ourselves inside.

A bored young boy approached his harried father with a common plea, "Dad, there's nothing to do."

As the father read the newspaper, he thought of a simple task that might keep his son busy. "Here, son, I've torn up this map of the world that was in today's paper. Why don't you take some tape and put it together?"

Thinking this would keep his son occupied for awhile,

the father returned to his paper. He was surprised when his son returned quite quickly with his project completed.

"How did you do this so fast?" the father asked.

"Simple," the boy replied. "There was a picture of a man on the back of the picture of the world. I just taped together the picture of the man, and when I got the man right, I got the world right."

Feel Good About Yourself

Bill Johnson was a downhill skier who made it to the Olympics in 1984. He was good, of course, but not considered to have a real chance. In fact, other skiers mocked his form and style. And, when it was time to begin the final run, Bill was in fourth place.

As he prepared to go down the slope, at what was quite possibly the most important moment of his life, he turned to his coach and said, "I hope all the great skiers in the world are watching me right now."

And then he won the gold by 1/100th of a second. Not one second. Nor 1/10th of a second. A mere 1/100th of a second was the difference on the clock that gave him the gold.

But the real difference was inside: the way he felt about himself, his feelings of self-respect and dignity.

Take the Challenge

How do we feel when we're faced with difficult challenges? Do we feel the confidence to perform as if the best in the world were watching us at that moment? Do we perform as we would if our children were viewing our performance?

Or do we shudder to face life's difficult assignments, and cling to the hope that we'll have smooth sailing for long periods of time?

Too many of us live just that way — hoping to avoid life's challenges and opportunities, just so we can avoid the potential hurdles, obstacles, and failures that inevitably occur when we take the field.

No one is successful all the time. It is only through our failures that we can appreciate our successes. And only through attempts that we can experience failure, the greatest teacher.

Don't be so afraid to fail as to be afraid to try.

When I was in high school, I dreamed of playing major league baseball. I was a poor fielder, which was not offset by my performance as a lousy hitter.

So, armed with a tremendous dose of "fear of failing so as not to look stupid," I didn't try out for the high school team.

The day of tryouts, I drove by the field, somewhat in envy of those who would soon be playing for the school. I saw the All-State pitcher from last year pitching to the new hopefuls.

He was pitching to Tommy.

Tommy was very small for his age and had a birth defect which made athletic activities hard for him.

He stood in the batting cage and swung mightily, but uselessly, at every pitch. His batting helmet was too big, his shorts were baggy, his bat was too big and heavy for him to swing.

He looked, I thought, somewhat foolish.

After a few pitches, the coach yelled, "That's enough, Kid." And Tommy replied, "Come on, Coach. Let me hit just one more."

Let him HIT just one more? Heck, he hadn't even come close to hitting the ball!

I started to laugh. And then I cried.

Tommy was out there giving the best he had trying to achieve.
I was on the sidelines watching, trying to avoid failing.

All of a sudden, Tommy didn't seem to appear so foolish . . .

In 25 years, I've never lost the feeling of respect I had that
day for Tommy.

Because, you see, Tommy got it right. Tommy knew that the
joy comes in trying to achieve. The challenge of life is to make
the attempt. Accomplishing tasks which we know we will master
before we begin is not a challenge.

The challenge comes when we attempt to perform tasks
which we are not sure we will accomplish.

And it is only through trying that we build self-respect.

Start a Life Project

One way to improve self-respect is to develop a Life Project.

A Life Project is the reason someone puts their feet on the
ground every morning, the reason that a person keeps going.

I have two: my sons and my message.

Due to the efforts of their mother, their uncles and aunts,
grandparents, teachers, friends, and myself, the world is a better place because of the presence of my two sons, Ted and
Wilson. Every day something is done on their behalf, if nothing
more than a prayer.

They are part of the focus of my life.

The other part of my Life Project is my message. Each year I
speak to thousands of people, knowing that if I can influence the
thoughts of a single person, a part of me has been left behind.

My sons and my message are my missions, my reasons for living. They are my Life Projects.

Each of us can find a Life Project. It can be as simple as a volunteer effort for a program we believe in. It can be our music, our art, our ability to teach. It can be our love.

Anything that we can give of ourselves, anything that causes us to focus on doing something for someone other than ourselves, anything that commands our attention every day — that is a Life Project.

A concert goer rushed up to famous violinist Van Cliburn following a performance and exclaimed, "I'd give my life to play like that."

"I did," was the maestro's reply.

Isn't it time for us to start on OUR Life Project?

Oliver Wendell Holmes said, "Most of us die with our music still in us."

Our Life Project turns simple tunes into symphonies. Our Life Project gives us dignity and self-respect. Feelings of self-worth which we then can share with others.

Developing My Life Project

These questions are intended to help get you started in developing your own Life Project. Let your thoughts run wild when answering them. Throw out conventional logic and open your mind as you answer the following:

1. What is it that I enjoy doing? (List as many things as you wish.)

2. Which of these can I do and help or share with someone else? (Teach, entertain, coach, support, etc.)

3. Where do I want to do it?

4. With whom? (Church, school, family, association, etc.)

5. What is keeping me from doing it now? (Be very specific here!)

6. How am I willing to change to complete my Life Project?

Find a Life Project. Find something other than work and television that gives you a reason to put your feet on the floor every morning when you wake up.

1

Silver Rule

The Rule of Difference:

We Must Celebrate, Not Resent, Different Styles

We Must Celebrate, Not Resent, Different Styles

"But, the great Master said, 'I see
No best in kind, but in degree;
I gave a various gift to each,
To charm, to strengthen, and to
teach.'"
— *Henry Wadsworth Longfellow*

One of the most important ideas that a good communicator can remember is that the world is blessed with different personality and behavior types. What a boring place this would be if everyone were the same!

As I'm writing this book, my youngest son, Wilson, plays center on his undefeated high school football team. When he first went out for football years ago, I wanted him to be a quarterback. After all, the quarterback gets the glory, the recognition, the headlines — they're the most important player on a team.

But I was wrong.

Watching Wilson play all these years, I've realized that a team won't win with eleven quarterbacks. It takes a mixture of different talents to have a winning season: linemen, backs, receivers. A championship team realizes the value of EVERY person on the team, and they celebrate their different skills and styles.

And just as a team with eleven quarterbacks won't win any football games, or a team of nine pitchers won't win in baseball, any team you're involved with, on the job or in life, where every personality and style is the same, is just as ineffective. Not to mention, much less fun!

Different Styles Bring Different Strengths

We must learn to celebrate people's different styles instead of resenting them and trying to make them be just like us.

Just because someone is slower to make a decision doesn't mean that the person doesn't understand the issue. It may mean their style is to evaluate things a little longer and a little more closely. They may be the ones who help "action heroes" make a better decision.

Similarly, there are times when a quick decision is vital to the success of a project or endeavor. It is then that the decisive, forceful personality is invaluable.

Behavioral scientists have determined that each of us has a predominant style which controls how we tend to do things.

Have you ever met someone for the first time where you felt a certain warmth, a sort of immediate bonding? And later, realizing that your style worked so well that time, you tried the same approach on someone else, only to feel like "we're not clicking?"

That's because one's natural style is more appealing to some behavioral types than it is to others. And it's not just you; everyone else is in the same situation, regardless of their own personal behavioral style.

Numerous behavioral studies performed over the past 20 years support the theory that we tend to behave in ways which can be categorized and even predicted to a certain degree, if we understand the different behavioral styles.

And once we understand the differences in people's styles, we can adapt our own style to "click" more effectively with different people.

Our challenge is to understand our own style while keeping in mind that it may be different from another person's style.

Different Behaviors Demand Different Needs

Different behavioral styles can be analogous to different animals.

Think about which of these animals might best describe you:

- Are you a LION? Forceful, decisive, competitive, logical, quick-thinking, dominant?
- Or maybe you are more like a PORPOISE? Playful, attention-grabbing, impulsive, interpersonal?
- Perhaps you are like a KOALA? Laid-back, easy-going, peace-loving, steady?
- Or maybe more like a FOX? Cunning, analytical, cautious?

Just as we would treat real lions, porpoises, koalas, and foxes differently, so we should communicate differently to individuals according to their dominant, playful, laid-back, or cautious behavioral styles.

By knowing our communication style, and understanding the characteristics of other styles, we can most likely "feed" different types in a way that will make them thrive.

For example, we can feed LIONS "to-the-point" communication since they make decisions so quickly. Because PORPOISES like small talk and chatter, we can feed them "stimulating and personal" communication. KOALAS like "sincere and steady" communication because they value relationships and security. And FOXES enjoy "information and data-filled" communication since they like to be informed.

Seminar attendee: "I resent that you keep putting people in boxes."

Seminar leader: "I don't put people in boxes. I just keep looking in boxes and finding people there."

How Do We Identify the Animal in Ourselves?

You might be asking how you can determine your own behavioral style of communication. Complete the "Guide to Anticipated Behavior" on page 12 to identify which of the four basic types of communication styles best describes you. You might already suspect what your style is, or you might be surprised. Either way, once you know your style, you can use that knowledge to improve your communication with others.

How Do We Identify the Animals in Others?

I recently visited the Memphis Zoo for the first time in years. I quickly noticed the signs in front of the different animals, which not only identified them, but included information about their preferences and behavioral tendencies.

Wouldn't it be wonderful if signs were in front of everyone's door or home with this same type of information? Imagine how helpful it would be to see a sign that said:

THIS IS A LION

It prefers to-the-point, bottom-line communication. It wants an environment where it can make decisions, be in charge, and have control.

WARNING: *The lion likes conflict and can be aggressive!*

Before we can feed the animals what they want, we need to identify them correctly. And we must understand a few principles before we begin.

First of all, these behavioral descriptions are tendencies, not absolutes. While all of us have a dominant behavioral style, most of us combine two or more styles. This means that we are actually combinations of these styles, but driven by one style alone.

Secondly, we change styles due to our environment. For example, we might be more forceful and decisive at work and more laid-back and steady at home. Or vice versa.

However, experience, as well as science, shows that we are all pretty predictable when it comes to how we behave and communicate. And we can predict pretty accurately if we know the style of the other person — if we know what type of animal they are.

So how can we identify these different styles?

We could ask everyone we meet to complete the "Guide to Anticipated Behavior" (pg. 12) found in this book.

This would allow us to study how they tend to act and know how to "feed" them appropriately. And while this actually works quite well, as a number of my clients can attest, this is not very reasonable to expect in our overall contact with people.

Another way is through observing another person's behavior and actions. We can pretty closely identify their style through their normal actions, behavior, and communication style.

And I can attest that with continued practice and effort, one can become rather accurate in their style estimates.

The following table shows how observations can help identify the styles:

STYLE	TENDENCIES	STYLE	TENDENCIES
LION	• Direct talker • Firm handshake • Steady eye contact • Blunt speaker • Fast talker • Authoritative dresser • Bottom-line orientation • Likes to be in charge	KOALA	• Good listener • Gentle handshake • Conservative dresser • Quiet volume • Slower moving • Reserves opinion • Likes security and status quo
PORPOISE	• Friendly • Talkative • Uses inflection and drama • Much hand and body movement • Likes contact • Bright or noticeable clothing • Likes to be noticed	FOX	• Asks instead of tells • Neat dresser • Fact oriented • Fewer gestures • Lower volume • Fewer facial expressions • Likes formality

By observing these signs, we can come fairly close to quickly anticipating the behavior of most of the people we deal with.

And this is important to attempt.

By treating everyone the same way, we are going to conflict with a fair number of styles. So even if we predict incorrectly, our chances of improving communication are no worse than if we stuck to our usual style.

Communication is one instance where "I just want to be me" doesn't work.

We must adapt.

I was called in to do some team building with a successful business systems organization. The company was very marketing-driven and the senior management consisted of a combination of LIONS and PORPOISES. Driven, active, expressive, competitive, and "rah-rah;" all of the ingredients one might expect in a high-powered sales organization.

However, the Chief Financial Officer was a FOX. Lower-keyed and not as expressive or vocal.

He was often uncomfortable around the others because he felt pressured and stressed to try to be more like them. They likewise often took his questioning and low-key style as an indication of lack of support for their ideas and criticism of the way they ran the company.

He experienced great relief when they all learned together that THIS WAS HIS STYLE — and they learned that his style was exactly what was needed in that role. Someone who would challenge them regularly with questions, while at the same time keeping close reins over the details of the company.

He saw his strengths and soon eliminated the pressure to be like the others.

They all learned to celebrate the differences.

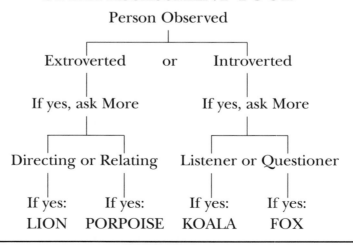

A QUICK COMMUNICATION STYLE ASSESSMENT TOOL

Person Observed

Extroverted   or   Introverted

If yes, ask More   If yes, ask More

Directing or Relating   Listener or Questioner

If yes:	If yes:	If yes:	If yes:
LION	PORPOISE	KOALA	FOX

Understand How Your Behavioral Style Works

My purpose here is not to simplify or minimize the complex science of behavior, but rather to encourage you to begin a process of understanding your own behavioral style and realizing that it is often different than the style of the person to whom you are speaking.

Sometimes the differences complement, sometimes they conflict. Adapting can minimize or eliminate the conflict. And it could make good relationships even better.

In every instance, difference is good. However, we can adapt our styles to become appealing to people of any behavioral type.

Recently, a woman at one of my seminars stated that she was having a particular problem with one of her co-workers — a person who displayed a dominant, forceful personality. Once she gained an understanding of her own behavioral style and was able to identify the style of her co-worker, she was able to make some adjustments in the way she communicated with the difficult co-worker. With great enthusiasm, she related that not only had she made a dramatic improvement in their communication and their relationship, but that her boss had noticed it as well and complimented her on her efforts. Her "understanding" was showing, and others could see it!

What Appeals to the Animals in People?

LIONS *like power.*

> *Feed them quick, bottom-line communication.*
> *Celebrate their leadership.*
> *Let them make decisions.*
> *Beware of their tendencies toward conflict.*

PORPOISES *like personality.*

> *Feed them stimulating, upbeat communication.*
> *Celebrate their enthusiasm.*
> *Let them tell their stories, dream their dreams, and digress.*
> *Beware of their tendencies toward emotional communication.*

KOALAS *like peace.*

> *Feed them predictability, steadiness, and patience.*
> *Celebrate their team spirit.*
> *Let them be deliberate and slower.*
> *Beware of their tendencies toward indecision and lack of expression.*

FOXES *like perfection.*

> *Feed them precise and formal communication.*
> *Celebrate their adherence to standards.*
> *Let them ask questions and take time to ponder.*
> *Beware of their tendencies toward over-perfection and nit-picking.*

Show a Little Understanding for Other Styles

That is where the first Silver Rule comes into play — understanding that the other person's style, and their needs, may be different from yours.

Treat the person you're communicating with the way they wish to be treated at that time, and celebrate the difference in style instead of resenting it!

> *All these LIONS, PORPOISES, KOALAS, and FOXES are really human beings.*
>
> *Feed them courtesy, dignity, and respect.*
>
> *Celebrate their differences.*
>
> *Let them be themselves and feel their individual feelings.*
>
> *Beware of their tendencies to respond with kindness when treated with kindness.*

And while we're celebrating the differences in behavioral styles, maybe it's time to celebrate the differences in other areas of life as well. Celebrate the differences in age, gender, race, education, and lifestyles. All these differences add up to a more diverse "team" with broader skills and understanding.

World-class communicators don't let differences stand in the way of communication. They celebrate the differences with dignity, respect, and understanding.

Guide to Anticipated Behavior

Research into behavior and communication has indicated there are four dominant communication styles. These styles describe the way individuals tend to communicate and behave in specific circumstances.

Instructions: Look at each row of adjectives across the page. Determine which word best describes you as you see yourself (not as you would like to be seen or think you are seen by others). Place a "4" next to this word. Then place a "3" beside the next most descriptive word, a "2" beside one of the remaining words which describes you, and a "1" next to the final word, which is the one you feel least describes you.

Example: _4_ Powerful _1_ Influential _2_ Stable _3_ Calculating

There should be no ties. Be as honest and brief in deciding as you can. Your first choice is usually your most accurate.

Remember this: there are no right or wrong answers, no best styles. We need all types in our world, our lives, and our work. Celebrate the difference!

Column A	Column B	Column C	Column D
___ Powerful	___ Influential	___ Stable	___ Calculating
___ Fearless	___ Upbeat	___ Methodical	___ Hesitant
___ Confident	___ Effervescent	___ Calm	___ Rational
___ Heroic	___ Welcoming	___ Steadying	___ Analytical
___ Impatient	___ Spontaneous	___ Protective	___ Accurate
___ Determined	___ Excitable	___ Agreeable	___ Skeptical
___ Dominant	___ Convincing	___ Unassuming	___ Inquisitive
___ Competitive	___ Verbose	___ Faithful	___ Clever
___ Explorative	___ Social	___ Laid-back	___ Particular
___ Vigorous	___ Personable	___ Peaceful	___ Constant
___ TOTAL	___ TOTAL	___ TOTAL	___ TOTAL

Add up the numbers in each vertical column. Total points per "animal" will display your general behavioral tendencies. The higher the total, the stronger the tendency.

COLUMN A	COLUMN B	COLUMN C	COLUMN D
LIONS_____	PORPOISES_____	KOALAS_____	FOXES_____

REMEMBER THIS:

The Good Lord, in His infinite wisdom, did a wonderful job of making us different. This would be a truly boring world if everyone were just alike.

Our challenge is to recognize and celebrate these differences. Whether they are racial, sexual, age, or cultural. We begin this by understanding our own style of behavior, with its strengths and limitations, and adapting our style to best communicate with others.

HOW TO USE THE RULE OF DIFFERENCE

1. Identify your personal communication style by completing the "Guide to Anticipated Behavior" found on page 12.

2. Learn how to identify the other person's style (LION, PORPOISE, KOALA, or FOX). Do this through observation or completion of the "Guide to Anticipated Behavior" as you observe the other person.

3. Modify your own style to complement the other person's style. This is done by providing the type of communication that "feeds" the other person's preference.

4. Observe closely the effect your changes in communication style are having on the other person and how they are being received, remembering that most of us combine two styles.

5. Shift your communication style toward the style that is being best received. These styles could be described as bottom-line (LION), personable (PORPOISE), sincere (KOALA), or cautious (FOX).

6. Practice The Rule of Difference on EVERYONE with whom you communicate.

Silver Rule

The Rule of Agendas:

We Must Recognize the
Other Person's Agendas

We Must Recognize the Other Person's Agendas

"The supreme value is not the future but the present . . . what a man truly wants he wants now."
— *Octavio Paz*

Just as everyone has a mental picture of themselves, everyone has two kinds of agendas.

One of these is a mental list of what a person is doing at a particular time.

This is their secondary agenda. Secondary agendas are dynamic. They change often.

And each secondary agenda is part of a larger, primary agenda. The primary agenda each of us carries exerts more control on us, largely dictating why we do what we do in the big picture.

It is sometimes called our motivation.

If we could read another person's agenda ("Here is what I'm doing and why I am doing it"), we could communicate and behave in a manner that would support or complement that agenda. We'd know when to step in and help, and when to get out of the way. We'd know when to tell a joke, and when to get serious. We'd know when to ask questions, and when to give advice.

But we don't pass our agendas around. We just assume that everybody else knows what our agendas are and will treat us accordingly.

Sometimes people help us with our agendas. Sometimes they get in our way, causing conflict. In either case, their actions could be purely accidental or based on personal insight. But they aren't necessarily based on a knowledge of our agendas.

There's an Agenda for Every Style

The different communication styles all have different agendas. If we know the other person's style, we can identify the broad strokes of their agenda with reasonable accuracy.

The LION's agenda is the task at hand. It is fairly safe to assume that their first priority is going to be whatever they are working on at that moment. Knowing this, we want to communicate in a way that causes them little interruption or aids them in finishing their task.

If we can identify which of the LION's tasks are important at the moment, we can get in sync with the LION. Likewise, if we have different agendas when we interface, we'll have difficulty communicating effectively.

The PORPOISE's agenda is different from the LION. The PORPOISE is motivated by self-approval. Their agenda will be not as focused on what they are working on as it is gaining your approval and recognition.

Just by these two examples, we can see how different agendas can cause conflict and poor communication.

The LION wants to work on the task. The PORPOISE comes into the picture wanting some recognition. This comes in the form of small talk. The LION doesn't want to slow down and visit. The PORPOISE is upset by the LION's snub. Neither one of their needs are met. Communication isn't good.

The KOALA's agenda is teamwork and status quo. They like peace and calmness, so they are motivated by things staying pretty much the same way, unless careful analysis shows how change could bring improvement.

Think about how the different agendas of the KOALA and LION might mix.

The LION likes change; give them a few logical facts and you'll see things changing fast. Compare that to the agenda of the KOALA: let's slow things down! The LION wants action, the KOALA wants to move slower. The LION needs results, the KOALA needs support. Different agendas. Result . . . conflict.

Then there's the agenda of the FOX — accuracy and procedure. They are motivated by correctness, the proper way of doing things.

Imagine how the different agendas of the PORPOISE and FOX might mix.

The PORPOISE, motivated by spontaneity and impulsive decision making, doesn't see much need for planning; let's just go! The FOX needs time to think and plan. Their agenda requires lots of information, plenty of facts.

If these two were traveling together without understanding each other's needs, imagine what would happen. The FOX would want to plan every step and couldn't understand how the PORPOISE could just go without more information. The PORPOISE would feel the FOX was spoiling all the fun by taking all the spontaneity out of the trip.

By knowing what is typically at the top of the other person's agenda, we can support that agenda and achieve effective communication. Without knowing and supporting another's agenda, we too often create conflict.

Everyone's Agenda Puts Themselves First

There is another important aspect of agendas: everyone's agenda has them at the top of the page. Oh, there are a few exceptions — times of crisis and a few unbelievably altruistic people, but most of the time everyone puts themselves first.

Others may be close to the top. A person's company might be very close to the top. Children might be close to the top.

But generally, #1 is number one.

This means we want to communicate their way for their benefit. They are doing things for their reasons, not ours.

Once we support their agenda in their way, we can have effective communication.

My secondary agenda at this writing is to complete this manuscript. Anybody communicating with me right now that supports this mission will have good communication with me.

An interruption that is brief and to the point will not cause conflict.

A call from my editor will not cause conflict.

An interruption for small talk will cause problems. That's not on my agenda right now. But Monday, after a football weekend, I might have small talk on my mind. That will be on my agenda then.

And my primary agenda in both instances is me; I am the central character in both agendas.

And with no uncertain amount of selfishness, if your agendas are consistent with mine, we communicate.

The problem comes with inconsistent agendas.

Primary Agendas Affect All Kinds of Decisions

Let's see how primary and secondary agendas would affect a business decision and how our knowledge of the Rule of Agendas helps us when we're selling to different styles.

The prospect has a need for a new computer. We are the computer sales representative. No matter what type of person we're dealing with, the secondary agenda is "buy a new computer system."

But the primary agenda for each behavioral style is different.

For example, the LION's primary agenda is to complete the task effectively. By recognizing this, we can aim our efforts towards getting the job done quickly, effectively, and on time. LIONS really appreciate our giving them fast responses, providing plenty of options, letting them make quick decisions, and getting out of the way. All these actions support the effectiveness requirement, which is the primary agenda of the LION.

The PORPOISE's primary agenda is approval. We want to show them how they can achieve approval and recognition by doing business with us. PORPOISES want to know that they will be mentioned in the newsletter, that we'll bring the executives of our firm in to meet them for dinner, that we'll let their boss know how effective they were to deal with, etc. All these actions support the approval requirement, which is the primary agenda of the PORPOISE.

The KOALA's primary agenda is stability. We want to show them how they can achieve stability and security by doing business with us. We will assure minimum interruption during the installation and show them how this will be done. We will introduce the team which will handle the installation and show them how they are prepared to respond to problems. All these actions support the stability requirement, which is the primary agenda of the KOALA.

The FOX's primary agenda is accuracy. We want to give them plenty of data and information on our product and services and give them plenty of time to think about it. We want to be unaggressive in our approach and selling. We want to be accurate in our proposal and numbers. All these actions support the accuracy requirement, which is the primary agenda of the FOX.

But in each case, the end result was the same — a new computer. Same result, different reasons. Different agendas.

Making Agendas Work for You

The key to using The Rule of Agendas effectively is to be aware that the other person's agenda at a particular time is more than likely different from your agenda at the same time.

I want to talk about the trip, but you want to finish your work. Different agendas.

I want the team to excel, but you want to be the star. Different agendas.

I want a lot of detail, but you want a quick summary. Different agendas.

So what do we do? Simple. We get on the other person's agenda.

We can only use agendas to further good communication when one of the parties is willing to meet the other person's agenda. Unless both agendas are miraculously the same thing at the same time.

Pete is a friend of mine. He is a PORPOISE, and he coaches football at a local high school.

One of the players on the team is a good kid named Frank. Frank is a KOALA, and last year he was the starting tailback.

Frank's dad is a LION, and he wants to see Frank play. That is his task, his mission, his primary agenda.

At the beginning of the season, everyone got along fine: Frank (the KOALA) was part of the team, Frank's dad (the LION) got to see him play every game and Pete (the PORPOISE) was well-liked by both of them. Their agendas were similar enough that everyone was communicating well.

Then, for the good of the team, Pete made Frank a back-up player.

Frank, the team player, needed to be talked to, reassured, made to understand he was still a team player. But Pete, because he was afraid of harming the relationship, avoided the conflict. And, of course, Frank's dad was not happy to see his task wasn't being accomplished — that his son was on the sidelines.

As Frank's playing time got less and less, the agenda differences began to show. The same communication styles that had worked earlier broke down.

Frank's dad couldn't get his task done — Frank wasn't playing — so he wasn't happy with Pete.

Pete was increasingly unpopular with Frank's dad and Frank. He was hurt and bothered.

Frank didn't feel like he was part of the team; he felt unappreciated. He wanted to quit.

No one bothered to get the other person's agenda.

But then Pete did something special.

He risked his primary agenda (approval) to support the agendas of Frank and Frank's dad, which were peace and power.

First, Pete met with Frank and told him how valuable he was to the team, whether as starter or back-up. He explained how much Frank was appreciated, how he was an important element of the entire unit. He was wanted.

Then Pete met with Frank's dad and requested help in solving the problem: the team had two talented players, but only one could start.

Pete gave Frank's dad options (remember, LIONS like to make decisions). Pete suggested Frank's dad either could support the decision that Frank play back-up, or that Frank could quit, or that Pete could make sure Frank got ample opportunity to practice and play occasionally with the first unit. He even offered to meet with Frank's dad to measure Frank's progress. He did this with an attitude of sincere interest and support of Frank.

The end result was good.

Pete's primary agenda of approval was met and his secondary agenda of building a winning team was supported.

Frank's primary agenda of peace and teamwork were met when he felt a part of the team.

And Frank's dad met his primary agenda of power — he was "in charge" helping his son.

Pete was able to read the different agendas, his included, and make sure they were all supported.

Whenever we're not comfortable identifying another person's style, or when we can't tell by observation what another person's agenda is, there's a simple, one-step way to find out for sure.

Ask.

"What's important to you right now? What is going on that I can help you with?"

Ask and observe. Ask what is important right now. (It will change constantly.) And observe how your efforts to support the other person's agenda affects your communication.

Practice this with the people whose relationships matter to you. And practice it every day.

REMEMBER THIS:

Every communication style has its own way of approaching its agenda, but for virtually everybody, the most important item on their agendas is themselves.

Get on the same agenda with them and communication will be improved.

HOW TO USE THE RULE OF AGENDAS

1. After identifying the other person's style, identify their primary agenda (LIONS = effectiveness and power, PORPOISES = approval and personality, KOALAS = stability and peace, FOXES = accuracy and perfection).

2. Identify the other person's secondary agenda. This is usually what task or objective is driving them at that particular time.

3. If this is not easily identified ask, "What is important to you right now?"

4. Then, attempt to support both agendas with your communication style.

Silver Rule

The Rule of Regard:

We Must Show Our Regard During
the First 45 Seconds of Contact

We Must Show Our Regard During the First 45 Seconds of Contact

---

"I ne'er could any luster see
In eyes that would not look on me."
— Richard Brinsley Sheridan

Whether we're speaking to one person or to a thousand, one good way to build a relationship is to look your audience in the eye.

See Eye-to-Eye With Your Audience

Looking our listeners "in the eye" accomplishes a number of things.

It shows confidence. Steady eye contact shows that the speaker (or the listener, for that matter) is comfortable with what is being said. It is perceived as a sort of litmus test for honesty. It answers the unspoken challenge "Can you look me in the eye and tell me that?"

Establishing eye contact shows we are listening. That we are concentrating on the other person and NOTHING else. Glancing away or looking elsewhere indicates distraction or a focus on something or someone else.

Eye contact shows we care. We tend to watch what we are interested in. Good eye contact displays a concentration on what is being said and communicates this interest to the other person.

Making Eye Contact Can Be a Challenge

Have you ever noticed how difficult it is to talk with someone in the front seat of a car when you are in the back seat and they're not looking in your direction?

This is an everyday example of how much eye contact adds to a conversation. More can be communicated by a glance or a glare than an entire conversation. Unfortunately, many people have developed a tendency to avoid eye contact during a conversation.

There are a couple of reasons for this.

People begin to avoid making eye contact because of the discomfort they have felt when they made eye contact during a moment of conflict. An individual can feel so much tension and discomfort in a situation like that, they start to build a habit of not making eye contact in order to avoid those uncomfortable feelings.

The other reason is that we just develop the bad habit of not looking our listener in the eye and then never correct it.

Poor Eye Contact Sends the Wrong Message

We must be aware of the signals that poor eye contact sends:
- Lack of confidence.
- Lack of belief in our message.
- Intimidation by the other person.

And just as making eye contact sends vital signals to the listener, the listener is sending vital signals back to the speaker through their eyes.

By looking into a listener's eyes, a speaker can get the answer to questions such as "Are you listening?" "Do you understand what I'm saying?" "Do you care about what I'm saying?"

All the answers to these questions, and even more, are conveyed without a word . . . through the eyes.

But how can we get these signals if we're not watching?

Improve Your Eye Contact

People who have trouble maintaining eye contact can try this exercise to improve their communication effectiveness.

As you listen to the other person, try to maintain a constant focus on that person's eyes "mirroring" the facial expression of the speaker.

When you speak, shift your gaze from their eyes to their ears or another nearby facial feature (don't shift your gaze to any exceptional features, however, as this would send an entirely different, and unwelcome, message).

As you continue the exercise, gradually shift your gaze closer to the listener's eyes and, once you reach the eyes, hold your eye contact.

Improved eye contact will send a message, loud and clear, of confidence, interest, and empathy.

Eye Contact Even Works in a Group

Steady eye contact is a requirement for any world-class presentation to a group as well.

When addressing a group, we should talk to the audience as if there were only two or three people in the room, pausing as we speak to make eye contact with the entire group.

While it is impossible to make eye contact with everyone in large audiences, the feeling that is projected is one of talking to individuals, not to an anonymous mob of bodies.

Call Them by Name

Another good way to establish a good rapport with another person is by using their name.

No word is as sweet to an individual as their name.

It is a gift from their parents to them, one that no one shares. We can "sweeten" our communication by using the listener's name on a regular basis. It reminds them that they are the sole focus of our interest at that moment.

Let me note that there are lines we should not cross which take us from courtesy into demeaning patronage when we overuse someone's name.

Corrie ten Boom, author of The Hiding Place, *tells the story of meeting an elderly woman for the first time.*

After a moment, ten Boom said, "I'm sorry, I've forgotten your name."

The woman smiled kindly and said, "That's all right . . . when someone is introduced, the only name they usually hear is their own."

I am reminded of this often when watching infomercials on television, specifically the ones which sell new "wonder" products.

These scenes often involve the host, with a name like "Don," who plays the role of an amazed straight man to the inventor of a wonder product, such as a mop which will suck up a small lake.

The huckster . . . er, inventor, usually refers to "Don" by name around four or five times per minute, by which time we are totally sick of both parties in the conversation.

This type of overuse is irritating and patronizing.

We want to use the other person's name in a manner that lets them know we know, and appreciate, who they are in a courteous, thoughtful manner.

When saying another person's name, make sure that your tone of voice avoids sounding condescending or superior. Instead, use the person's name frequently in respectful tones and notice the continued interest they will have in what you are saying.

Making Contact

In the first 45 seconds we're with someone, we show our regard or disregard.

These are the ways we show regard:

- Smiling when you see them.
- Using their name and looking them in the eye.
- Asking a question that shows your interest: "Are you new to the company?" "Did you see the game last night?"
- Following their lead. LIONS may be busy, PORPOISES talk, KOALAS listen, FOXES may be brief.
- Sincerely acting as if you are glad to see them.

These are the ways we show disregard:

- Don't look them in the eye.
- Walk past without acknowledgment.
- Don't listen when they speak to you.
- Act as if your problem is bigger than theirs.

Take a second now and evaluate how you typically show your regard for others during the day.

Follow these tips and see how people treat you the next time you see them!

Use Nicknames Carefully

Unless you are close to a person, be extremely careful about using nicknames or familiar names without being invited to do so.

I met a gentleman during a recent assignment named Dan. Dan was always gregarious and fun to speak to whenever I saw him. As we would begin to chat more and more, I called him "Danny" on more than one occasion. ("Morning, Danny. How's it going?")

One day Danny walked by me without speaking. I figured he must have a lot on his mind and let him pass.

Later, I passed him again. Again, no comment.

A few days later, the same thing occurred.

The next time I saw Danny, I stopped and told him I had noticed that he seemed somewhat aloof when I was around, and I wondered if something had occurred in our previous conversations that had offended him.

He told me simply, "I don't like being called Danny. It goes back a long way, but I don't like it. I would just as soon not be around you if you are going to call me that."

After a simple "I understand how you feel. It won't happen again," Danny became Dan again and all was well.

A good lesson learned.

REMEMBER THIS:

The more we acknowledge the importance of the other person, the more we enhance the effectiveness of our own communication.

Affirming others through such simple means as looking them in the eye when we speak and using their names to address them goes far in making our audience more receptive to our communication.

HOW TO USE THE RULE OF REGARD

1. When greeting a person, look them in the eye as you speak. Maintain this eye contact during your conversation.

2. In your conversation, use their name. If unsure about their name, ask for it. Most people are forgiving if you make your request with a comment such as, "I am so bad with names . . . what is your name again?"

3. Ask something which implies your sincere interest in them. "Did your daughter's soccer team win yesterday?" "Tell me about your meeting Wednesday.", etc.

4. Smile.

5. If approached with a problem, remember that their problem is probably just as important to them at that moment as yours are to you. They simply need someone to listen and help.

6. Observe the way people begin to treat you when they first see you after you have practiced this rule.

4

Silver Rule

The Rule of Empathy:

We Must Show We Care for
the Other Person's Situation

We Must Show We Care for the Other Person's Situation

"To understand everything makes one tolerant."

— *Germaine de Stael*

People want to be understood.

They want to deal with someone who understands their problems, their fears, their worries, the "stuff" they carry around with them every day.

They keep coming back to the people and the companies, who say with their actions and their attitude, "I understand . . . I want to help."

People Seek Out Others Who Understand Them

Alcoholics Anonymous, divorce recovery workshops, Mothers Against Drunk Driving — all of these support groups and hundreds more are popular because people can surround themselves with others who have "been there," people who understand what is going on, people who can empathize with their situation and their feelings . . . people who have shared the same experiences.

Customers, prospects, family members, virtually everyone will go out of their way to be around people who understand them. And they will avoid those who show that they don't.

Do you really want to spend time with someone who says (either verbally or nonverbally), "I don't care about you or your problems?"

I can remember as a child having problems at school or with friends. I would go to my mother, who would comfort me by telling me that she had been there, that she understood, and that it was all going to be all right.

That's empathy. The warmth of a mother's arms, a feeling that is communicated as "I understand . . . I care . . . I've been there." Parents tend to empathize with children.

It is time for employers to empathize with employees, for companies to empathize with customers.

Take a look at the annual lists of companies who make up the 100 best places to work. You'll find examples of firms who understand the needs of single parents, people facing retirement, employees who want to further their education, and much more. Someone at those companies has said, "I understand their dilemma, let's do something about it."

Someone empathized.

Put Yourself in the Other Person's Shoes

People are drawn to people who empathize. You should strive to show your empathy every time you communicate.

The secret to empathy is to actually "thrust" yourself into whatever the other person must be feeling at that time, to put yourself in the other person's shoes emotionally.

The nicest compliment that can be paid:
"I feel better about myself when I am with you."

Effective empathy is a two-way street: it comes in as a feeling of understanding for the other person and then this feeling of understanding is returned in effective communication.

A recent article in *USA Today* concerning sexual harassment in public schools had this quote: "We know that underlying a lot of this (sexual harassment) is a basic lack of empathy among children," says Joan Cole Duffell, director of community education for the Committee for Children in Seattle. "Many, many children are being raised with a real lack of social skills, and one of the most critical is the ability to empathize. Sexual harassment is just one example of how that's manifested in school."

Every time you communicate with someone, you display your empathy, or lack of it, for them. From the secretary you first see in the morning to the Chairman of the Board, from your child to your spouse, every time you communicate you state clearly whether or not you are "tuned in" to that person.

At some point during my Management Communication seminars, I ask whether the attendees feel that their superiors empathize with them. The answer is usually disappointing — an overwhelming "NO!" This lack of empathy is reflected in not having time to help, giving a feeling of "Not now, my problem is bigger than yours. My problem affects the whole company!"

Lack of empathy is also reflected by those who can't find time to occasionally stroke an employee, or give a little word of appreciation or encouragement for a tough task.

Check Your Empathy Level

How do we know whether we communicate empathy or not? Check your empathy level by asking yourself these questions:
- Do I show that I am listening to the other person?
- Does my body language indicate that I am interested in what is being said?
- Does my tone of voice reflect interest or understanding of the other person?
- Do I acknowledge what is being said to me?
- Do I indicate an appreciation of what the other person is experiencing?

- Do I indicate a willingness to learn more, even just a little more, about what the other person is experiencing?

If you answer NO to these questions, don't expect to get selected as "Manager of the Year" by your employees at the next annual banquet.

Different Behavioral Styles Show Empathy in Different Ways

When we're attempting to convey empathy, we must remember that our personal behavioral styles affect the ways we tend to show our interest. Sometimes those styles will be misunderstood by the people we're trying to show empathy with.

For example, a LION may tend to give advice, thinking that is what the person with the problem needs.

The PORPOISE may tend to use enthusiasm and encouragement to aid with problems.

The KOALA may lean towards sincere listening and calmness.

And the FOX may ask questions for clarification and details.

Each of these are legitimate efforts (according to the behavioral style involved) to show concern and empathy for another's problems. And in most cases, a sincere attitude of concern speaks louder than the words.

But the direct LION could be more effective by listening more and giving less advice (unless asked).

The talkative PORPOISE could try to listen more and give less superficial encouragement, especially to KOALAS and FOXES.

The laid-back KOALA could take a more active role.

And the cautious FOX could try to ask fewer questions and be less critical.

Everyone Has Problems

Have you ever known anyone without problems? If you think you do, think again. Everyone has them. They are just different than yours.

Some of you reading this book might be dealing with severe health problems. Others could be experiencing problems in relationships. Still more are suffering from enormous financial pressures. When it comes to problems, everyone has at least one.

Remember PEZ candy dispensers? The ones that stack the little candy pieces so that when you pulled one out, another one moves up to take its place at the top?

Troubles are like that PEZ candy: deal with one and another one comes to the top.

The problem at the top of the other guy's PEZ is as important to him as the problem at the top of your PEZ. When we communicate non-empathetically, we say, "My problems are more important than yours."

Nothing could be further from the truth.

In the eyes of the other guy, his or her problems are at the top, not yours.

Check Your PEZ . . . and Theirs

My staff assistant will occasionally catch me not paying full attention to something she is saying. When she does, she flicks her thumb in her fist, to remind me of the PEZ. In effect, what she is saying is, "Hey! My problems right now are as important to me as your problems and I need help!" She's right and it works.

It's time to check our PEZ and remember the other person's PEZ as well.

Our problems and concerns are all different. What's at the top of our concerns could be way down the stack for someone else. While one person's main concern may be getting a job done fast, another person could consider the cost of finishing the job as far more important. For effective communication, both these concerns need to be understood and empathized with.

Be Thankful for the Problems You Have

Incidentally, keep in mind that many of the problems which find their way to the top of our PEZ are the problems of Kings.

The roof is leaking and will cost money to repair. Thank goodness for the roof; 95% of the world wishes they were well-housed enough to even have a problem like that. The same thing goes for stalled cars, outgrown clothes, and cold pizza.

Be thankful for the opportunities to have those problems.

Most of us are so fortunate, we don't know what problems really are.

REMEMBER THIS:

People are drawn to individuals who can relate to their circumstances. Every time we communicate, we reflect our empathy for the other person. Whether it's in person or on the telephone, one-on-one or to a group, our empathy shows!

Check your empathy level the next time you talk to someone. In fact, check it every time.

HOW TO USE THE RULE OF EMPATHY

1. Remember that behind every set of eyes we encounter, there are problems we can't see.

2. Remember that the other person's problems are bigger to them right now than yours are to you.

3. Maintain steady eye contact during the conversation to express your interest in what is said. No eye contact indicates no interest.

4. Mirror the expressions of the speaker. Nod when they nod, smile when they smile. Lean forward when significant points are made.

5. Ask questions to clarify what is being said and to verify your interest.

6. Eliminate distracting actions, such as looking at your watch or slouching down in your chair.

Silver Rule

The Rule of Listening:

We Must Listen as
Much as We Talk

We Must Listen as Much as We Talk

"A good listener is not only popular but after a while he knows something."

— *Wilson Mizner*

The number one complaint for customers is poor listening. The number one complaint in social communication is not being listened to.

Listening is the most important communication skill. In fact, it is number one on everyone's list.

When we empathize, we listen.

Hearing is Not Listening

Most of us are born with the tools necessary to hear. We hear things going around us constantly: the air conditioner, horns honking, birds chirping, other people talking. It comes naturally and we don't need much practice to do it well.

Listening is another thing altogether.

Listening is a learned skill, a skill that we can improve with practice and concentration. Good listeners are a refreshing addition to today's communication. Good listeners show one of the most important signs of empathy.

Fortunately, there are some simple steps we can take to improve our listening skills.

Train Your Ears to Listen

This means practice. Look the speaker in the eye and concentrate on what is being said. Promise yourself that you will focus on that conversation and block out everything else.

Keep doing it. It takes a lifetime of practice to be a great listener.

The #1 Complaint in Customer Service:
The #1 Complaint to Marriage Counselors:
The #1 Complaint Children have about Parents:
"They're not listening!"

Remember the Listening Speed Rule

There's a basic rule to every conversation: the person who is speaking talks much slower than the person who is listening thinks. This is why you can process so much more than what is being said at that point. And this is why we can easily be distracted if we aren't careful.

The secret here is concentration. Forget the other things on your mind and give your undivided thought to the person speaking.

Ask Questions to Aid in Concentration

In person-to-person communication, the individual who asks the most questions usually controls the conversation.

Questions cause the speaker to pause for an answer while giving the person asking the question time to think, reflect, and regroup for further conversation.

However, effective questioning can also improve one's ability to concentrate on the speaker. It reflects that you are listening to what is being said and interested in knowing more.

In a recent sales seminar, attendees were asked to role play and practice their questioning skills.

The results were interesting.

While the seminar participants were fairly effective in their questioning techniques, the questions they asked didn't probe, or take the presentation anywhere. In other words, the questions were just filling space, using time. They added nothing to the dialogue or the participants' mutual understanding of the issues. But by asking relevant questions, they could have learned more about each prospect's needs and enhanced the communication. As it was, they were simply taking up time.

Ask the Right Questions

Ineffective questioning can cause people we're communicating with to become defensive. Questions which imply a judgment is being made or that indicate idle curiosity are rarely taken positively by the other person.

Effective questions involve an attitude of interest and support. They in essence say, "I am asking questions due to my interest in your topic and my desire to support your endeavors."

A judgment-sounding question like "Are you going to use ALL that paper?" becomes much more supportive when it is expressed as "Do you need more paper?"

It is amazing how often disagreements begin because a question was asked that was perceived as judgmental or critical by the listener.

"Are you working late again tonight?" might better be phrased "Do you know about what time you will be home?"

People are more apt to answer questions when they are asked in an empathetic way that doesn't make them feel like they're facing an inquisition or on trial.

Here are several proven questioning techniques which I have found to be extremely effective:

Summary questions:
- "So what I'm hearing is . . . . "
- "As I understand what you're saying . . . . "

Probing questions:
- "What else should I be aware of?"
- "Tell me more."
- "Why is that?"

Empathy statements:
- "I can see this means a lot to you."
- "I sense you are feeling . . . . "
- "I understand how you feel."

Hold Up a Mirror When You're Listening

One of the best ways to show you are listening and acknowledging the other person's message is called mirroring.

Mirroring involves "reflecting" the message of the speaker through your body language. Examples of mirroring include nodding as the speaker makes points, leaning forward when the speaker leans, and using occasional verbal signals such as, "I understand," "I see," etc.

These mirroring signals simply reflect your understanding of what is being said.

Who doesn't want to be understood when they are telling their story? Mirroring confirms that the message is clearly received by reflecting the speaker's own message back to them.

My business partner recently came back from a meeting where he had the opportunity to meet the new 1994 Miss America, Heather Whitestone, who has been deaf since a young age.

In addition to being a charming person, this is how he described her.

"Ed, she listened with her eyes."

Listening Is Not Easy Work

Ask any counselor, disgruntled teenager, employee, or customer. You will probably find the most common complaint in communication is "They don't take the time to listen."

It takes time, practice, and a conscious effort to improve listening skills. But it's worth every minute of effort, because everyone loves a good listener.

Different Styles Listen in Different Ways

Just as we need to be aware of how the different styles communicate, we should also be aware that there are different styles of listening, too.

LIONS tend to be selective listeners. They pay attention to part of what is said and do not pay attention to the rest. They will interrupt, feeling they know the gist of the conversation by highlights of what has been said. They reach quick conclusions and wish others would "get to the point."

PORPOISES like to listen. And talk. They tend to listen only so they will be prepared to say something. They can give the impression that they are listening to make sure they have the speaker's approval, when actually they aren't listening at all. They laugh at your humor and cry at your sorrow. They love your personal stories.

KOALAS like to listen. And they are good at it. They sincerely take the time to hear your message and if the message is delivered with sincerity, they make the best and most loyal listeners. They may occasionally ask questions for clarification, but they tend to pretty much "listen up." While not as outwardly expressive as PORPOISES, they too will share in others' laughter and feelings.

FOXES listen, but critically. While not necessarily listening to make a judgment (though this is often the case), they are on a quest for information and will ask questions to get what they want. Their responses to listening will be "why" questions, aimed at getting more information. They don't like fluff and hot air. They want facts.

Stop Talking . . . Make Yourself Listen

"He who does not understand your silence will probably not understand your words."
— *Elbert Hubbard*

Silence can serve as an effective tool for a speaker during a conversation, a presentation, or even a speech.

It can be used to punctuate, emphasize, and, when used effectively, can be a strong tool to gain the attention of the listener.

In the last case, your silence actually makes the listener uncomfortable. Most listeners tend to wonder about a period of silence, thinking things such as "I wonder what he/she is thinking now?"

As the speaker during conversations, we can use silence to gain attention. This is especially true when addressing two or more people. When your audience is not paying attention, simply stop speaking while maintaining your positive body language and eye contact. This generates the clear message that you expect their attention before you continue speaking.

There is another good time to be quiet. It is when we don't have anything to say!

A brand new preacher was ready to deliver his first sermon when he noticed that only one church member was present: a local farmer.

"I've prepared a sermon," the preacher explained, "would you be so kind as to listen to it and let me know how I do?"

The farmer responded, "I'm a farmer. I don't know nothing about preaching. But I do know that if it was time for all the cows to be fed, but only one cow showed up, I'd feed it."

Encouraged, the minister began. And he concluded, two and a half hell-fire and brimstone-packed hours later. Then he asked the farmer's opinion.

"I'm a farmer. I don't know nothing about preaching. I do know that if it was time for all the cows to be fed, but only one cow showed up, I'd feed it.

"But I'd be danged if I'd feed it the full load."

As a coach to professional speakers, I have used a four-point checklist for my speakers to review before making any presentation. While I developed this list for platform presentations, it is also just as effective for personal or social conversations.

It can help change pontificating into meaningful dialogue.

The four questions to ask before any communication are:

1. What is my message or belief? What am I trying to convey?

2. What is the basis for my message? What qualifies me to talk about this? Is it experience, learning, observation, etc.?

3. Why is it important to the listener? Can I convey why I feel that this is something that they need to hear? (If not, maybe it is best not to speak at all!)

4. What do I want my listeners to do? Is there action to be taken?

The most important of the four questions is number 3.
Why is it important?
Maybe it's time to let other people talk until we have something to offer to them.

A wise person once said, "It is better to be silent and have people wonder if you are a fool than to speak and remove all doubt."

REMEMBER THIS:

Listening comes only with practice. Concentration, on both the speaker and the story being told, is the most important tip for good listening.

AND ALSO . . . REMEMBER THIS:

Silence is exceptionally eloquent. It can grab attention, focus thoughts, cause people to think in ways words never can.

HOW TO USE THE RULE OF LISTENING

1. Remember that listening must be practiced.
2. Concentrate on the words and actions of the speaker.
3. Listen to complete sentences before thinking of your response.
4. Acknowledge what is said through short, frequent responses such as "I see" "I understand," etc.
5. Ask questions for clarification, making sure these questions are for information and support, not judgment.
6. Eliminate your personal problems and distractions.
7. Maintain steady eye contact.

Silver Rule

The Rule of Respect:

We Must Show Respect for
the Other Person's Feelings

We Must Show Respect for the Other Person's Feelings

"To be capable of respect is almost as rare as to be worthy of it."
— *Joseph Joubert*

Defensive behavior destroys relationships.

It doesn't matter whether it's a business, customer, social, or family relationship, defensiveness will break it and destroy it.

Defensiveness comes as a result of a need to justify an action. This is a common problem in business; a customer has a problem and the customer service representative spends a lot of effort explaining the cause of the problem.

The customer doesn't care.

Don't Explain Problems — Solve Them

We're in business to solve problems, not explain them.

Beginning today, forget about explaining your actions and focus on solving the problems. It makes no difference whether your actions contributed to the problem or didn't . . . simply solve the problem and get on with things.

The way to begin the mission to solve any problem is to use these words when a problem is brought to your attention: "I understand how you feel."

Then solve the problem.

"Your service is terrible."
   "I understand how you feel."
"I will never do business with you again."
   "I understand how you feel."
"You are a lazy bum."
   "I understand how you feel."

In every case "I understand how you feel" is the response . . . and since we have all experienced the feelings of the speaker, we are always safe in stating that fact.

Change Minds by Actions — Not Words

Arguing will not change anyone's mind or solve their problems. Explaining or rationalizing will not help, either. And the fact that the statement the person is making may not be true is not important. What is important is that the speaker thinks their problem is valid. And should be solved.

When you say you understand how someone feels, you are agreeing with the feelings of the person, not the facts.

So don't waste time defending your actions, company policy, or the condition of the world. Solve the problem at hand.

That's when the mind of the other person gets changed — not as a result of your debating how they should or shouldn't feel.

You can explain and explain, and most of the time they will finally concur with you just to move on to other things! But you haven't changed their mind about how they feel . . . and you haven't solved their problem. So you shouldn't be surprised when you later discover they still have the same opinion. Only by then, it's probably gotten worse.

A couple of years ago, I was invited by another consultant to help with a problem.

The client was a large mortgage company. Twice a year they sent out statements to hundreds of thousands of customers. Obviously, this resulted in thousands of telephone calls with questions, complaints about escrow amounts, you name it. To handle the influx of calls, the mortgage company hired dozens of temporaries to help answer customer questions.

The consultant had done a thorough job of estimating the length of time these calls would take so the mortgage company would have enough telephone lines to handle the calls without inconveniencing their customers.

But when the calls started coming through, the length of the average call was much too long.

He asked me to help and we discovered the customer service people were explaining everything every time a customer had a problem!

"We're all temps" "We have a heavy abundance of calls" "We only send these twice a year" and on and on. These detailed explanations were causing the calls to be longer than planned, which caused longer delays than planned, which caused more customer complaints to explain! A real problem!

Through some non-defensive behavior training, we were able to teach the people answering the phones that the customers didn't care what was causing the problem, they just wanted help. Through the magic words, "I understand how you feel," they were able to get right to solving problems, which reduced the length of the calls and reduced complaints.

"I Understand" Is Not the Same as "I Apologize"

The practice of saying "I understand how you feel" creates a lot of discussion during my seminars. And it is important to practice this technique.

Here is the simple, but powerful, secret behind this non-defensive response to criticism: we can understand virtually any feeling which is reflected to us. Whether it's anger, fear, or loneliness; no matter what the feeling, you've experienced it.

But while we can understand the feeling, we may not understand, or agree with, the facts.

I don't think my company's service is terrible, but I've done business with companies which provided (to my mind) terrible service. So I can understand someone's feeling of dissatisfaction with service. If you feel that way, I can understand. Now, what can I do to solve your problems?

Take a look at this not-unusual response to a customer service complaint:

A customer calls with a billing complaint saying, "My telephone bill is incorrect again. This is the third time I've had to call about this. Can't you people straighten out just one little problem?"

And the telephone representative replies, "I'm sorry for the problem, ma'am. We've had computer problems and the new system is being debugged. It should be better next month and you probably won't have this problem in your next bill."

This is a polite response, but defensive.

First of all, the telephone representative doesn't need to apologize: he did nothing wrong! But many of us make excessive apologies when criticized. It's okay to apologize for the inconvenience, but you don't need to apologize for your actions (unless you caused the problem intentionally yourself).

Secondly, explaining the situation doesn't solve the problem. The solution is what is important to the caller, not the reason behind it.

Let's take that same example and try some non-defensive problem solving. I've highlighted the non-defensive responses by putting them in italics.

The customer calls the telephone company for the third time with a billing complaint. After listening, the telephone representative replies,

> *"I understand how you feel. I wouldn't want to call three times, either. What can I do to help?"*

See the difference? This time the representative agrees with the feelings of the customer and then goes straight to solving the problem.

Let's take the dialogue further and see how we can continue to be non-defensive even if the heat gets turned up a little. Keep your eyes open for the "can't/can technique."

In response to the representative's question about solving the problem, the customer says, "Well, you can begin by giving me credit for the last two months' bills since you can't seem to get them straight."

Of course, this is an impossible request to grant, but the telephone representative says,

> *"I understand your feeling that way. I'd probably want a credit myself. I can't give you credit. I can go immediately to accounting and correct the bill. Would that work?"*

Notice that the representative has once again agreed with the customer's complaint and has even asserted that he might feel the same way in that situation. The representative then offered a workable compromise, saying what they can't do followed by a statement of what they can do to solve the problem.

Suppose the customer continues to complain, "This is piti-ful. A company like yours, who claims to take care of customers, not giving a credit to a little customer who has been put out."

The representative would respond,

"I sense your dissatisfaction and understand. I can't give you a credit. What I can do is go directly to accounting and get this straight. Then I'm going to call you back and let you know we made the correction."

Because the representative sticks to this non-defensive prob-lem-solving technique, the customer finally gets the picture that the representative is not going to argue with her and wants to help. By agreeing with the feeling and continuing to offer compromise solutions, the two will finally agree to a resolution.

This technique can be tried with any criticism, both at work and at home.

For example, a client of mine had been trying for five weeks to collect on a $108,000 bill of one of their customers. At one of our seminars, we role-played the communication with this customer. After they tried it, they collected their money.

This is what happened:

My client, we'll call them the ABC Company, had installed a telephone system for their customer. There were a few minor parts missing which didn't affect performance, and ABC Company agreed to install them as soon as they came in. The customer (a LION) was angry, and he didn't want to pay at all.

ABC Company contacted the customer and said, "John, we have a problem. There is a $108,000 balance due on your account and we need to resolve it. What can we do to satisfy you and collect this balance?"

John, the customer, answered, "I'll tell you what to do: get the parts in."

"John, I understand how you feel. We'd like the parts in, too.

I can't get the parts for three weeks, but what I can do is get loaner parts until yours comes in. Would that work?"

"I feel like this: it's as if I had bought a green Cadillac and you delivered a white Cadillac. If I'd wanted a white one, I'd have ordered a white one."

ABC Company responded, "I understand that. I can't get the green Cadillac, but I can let you drive the white one until the green one comes in. Would that work?"

With that, the customer okayed the deal and paid the balance. After weeks of explaining and apologizing, it was simplified when non-defensive problem-solving techniques were used.

Don't Fight, Make it Right

Non-defensive behavior is like the name implies: I don't intend to fight. I intend to win by keeping control. (This is especially strong medicine for getting along with LIONS, who lean towards conflict . . . . PORPOISES, KOALAS, and FOXES all tend to avoid conflict.)

Non-defensive techniques can also be used assertively, such as when a request is made.

Consider this exchange I initiated at a restaurant where the service was poor and slow:

I asked for the manager and said, "This has not been a good experience. This was our first time here and the orders were incorrect and entirely too slow. I am not going to pay full price for this."

The manager replied, "I'm sorry. Your server is new and we have a large party in the other room."

I replied, "I understand how you feel. I'm sure it is busy. I'm not going to pay full price for this meal."

The manager continued, "I'm sorry the night was bad. It is not normally like this. There is nothing I can do."

"I understand how you feel. I'm not going to pay full price for this."

His response was, "Sir, I am really sorry. I wish this had been a better experience for you and your guests."

"I understand your concern. I'm sure this is not the normal service. I'm not going to pay full price for this," I replied.

At this point the manager turned to the server and said, "This gentleman's ticket is on the house."

The use of non-defensiveness in this case is combined with a repetitive request, sometimes called a broken record.

This type of response works much better than such commonplace statements as "I don't care if you're busy or not" or "I could care less about the new waitress." By seeing the point of view of the manager ("I understand how you feel"), and politely standing firm with the request ("I'm not paying full price for this"), a compromise is reached.

Please note that in this case I got more than I asked for. I would have accepted a discount; instead, I received a free evening. By asking me what he could do to solve my problem, the manager would have saved money. (Incidentally, it's only fair to note that in a case like this, offering a refund or credit, induces me to come back again, so the grantor of the credit anticipates getting a return on this investment.)

Sometimes people ask me if we won't start sounding silly saying "I understand how you feel" all the time. The answer is yes, we will.

So we need to learn a number of alternatives to use after we've stated our understanding one or two times.

"I understand that."

"I'm with you."

"I see your perspective."

"I can see it that way."

These should be used only after stating, "I understand how you feel."

Remember, we are not agreeing with facts. And we are not claiming to "know" how someone feels. We understand.

In fact, if someone comes back with "How could you know how I feel? You've never waited tables/answered phones/had a computer eat your files/etc." The response is "You're right. But I sensed your frustration/anger/sadness, and if that is what you're feeling, I understand that."

Defensive behavior:
- *Is a result of real or perceived criticism, often unspoken.*
- *Comes as a result of a need to justify our actions.*
- *Destroys relationships.*

We're Entitled to Our Feelings, Too

While we're talking about understanding the other person's feelings, let's not forget that we're entitled to our own feelings as well.

In his book, *When I Say No, I Feel Guilty,* Dr. Manuel Smith provides a list of ten assertive rights to which we are all entitled. I would like for you to pay close attention to three of these:

1. You have the right to judge your own behavior, thoughts, and emotion, and to take the responsibility for their initiation, and consequences, upon yourself.

2. You have the right to offer no reasons or excuses for justifying your behavior.

3. You have the right to make mistakes . . . and be responsible for them.

In other words, you and you alone are the judge of your actions and communication. You. Period.

For many of us, it is a tremendous relief when we finally accept this. We are not surrounded by real judges, just some people who have made themselves self-appointed judges.

You know them. They're identified by comments like "Why are you doing that?" "That's not the way to do that" "You shouldn't act that way."

Our decisions not to follow legal laws have specific consequences. Our decisions not to follow moral or religious laws have similar results. Our decisions not to do or say things the way someone else might do or say them have no consequences.

So do it your way.

In Your Own Space, Whatever You Feel Is OK

Volumes have been written regarding assertiveness versus passive or aggressive behavior, but the bottom line always comes out the same: as long as we stay in our own space, it is okay to be ourselves and feel whatever we want to feel.

It is okay to feel things like "I don't want to go to work today" "I wish I lived on the beach" "I hate this food I'm being served" "I don't think my spouse is funny" or "I wish my daughter weren't getting married."

In fact, any feeling you might be having is okay. It's really okay.

What might not be okay (or appropriate, or polite, or even legal in some instances) is to express or act out your feelings. It's okay to feel like punching out the guy smoking in the third row, but punching him out might land you in jail!

In other words, we should spend far less time feeling guilty for what we feel, and more time getting in touch with WHY we feel what we feel and if we want to change our feelings.

Know Your Space, and When to Protect It

Occasionally, we are going to get in someone else's "space." We should respect that person's right to tell us when we do.

When someone's personal space is invaded, it's okay for that person to say how they feel. Most of us, however, are reluctant to tell someone that an action he or she is taking is bothering us.

As I write this book, the current style of men's ties is colorful and flowery. I like them and have many just like that. But I have an associate who hates them.

Occasionally, he will comment on my tie: "I hate those ties! I would never wear one like that. I would never wear a tie that looks like it should be hung on a wall!"

Does he have the right to tell me that? Yes.

Should I be defensive? No. It is really not important that he approve of my attire. It is not his space.

But what if my tie were offensive, say, with a nude sketch or picture on it? Would I be in his space then?

Walking down the street, no (assuming we're not talking illegal pornography!). But on a joint business call, he would be well within his assertive rights to describe the feelings he has about my wearing an offensive tie when we are representing our firm.

The fine line that marks off someone else's space is often crossed without our being aware of it. It is important to recognize that person's right to assert themselves to protect their space just as we have the right to assert ourselves for our own space.

You Can Assert Yourself Without Being Judgmental

In his book, *People Skills*, Robert Bolton gives a good guide for effectively describing behavior in non-judgmental means.
1. Describe the behavior in specific rather that fuzzy terms. In other words, be very specific about the behavior that is caus-

ing your feelings. Don't use general terms like "When you ignore my instructions . . . ." Use specifics like "When you report to work late three times a week . . . ."

2. Limit yourself to behavioral description, avoiding inferences about motives, character, etc. Again, use specific descriptions like "When you cut people off before they are finished speaking . . . ," as opposed to "When you act rudely . . . ." Specifically describe the behavior, not what you think the motive might be.

3. Make your descriptions as brief as possible. There is no need to use needless words in the description of the behavior. Be brief, accurate, and to the point. Describe the behavior in stark clarity.

4. Be sure to assert about the real issues. Don't be vague or ambiguous. Describe the real issue, not some other topic that you feel more comfortable with.

When we get in someone else's space, expect to be told. When someone gets in our space, tell them!

Express yourself . . . let the world know what you feel.

Do it your way. There is room for individualism and different points of view.

Do it your way, with kindness, and watch the magnificent results.

Understanding Creates Kindness

Not surprisingly, when we begin to work at understanding feelings, we begin to make acts of kindness commonplace.

One of my favorite examples of this happened a few years ago at Gerber's, the baby food company.

Gerber's decided to discontinue a particular type of baby food formula — a meat-based formula. They went about all the proper research and communication to sales, the Board, employees, and the marketplace to announce that this food item would no longer be made.

This created a problem for Raymond Dunn Jr., and his mother.

Raymond Dunn Jr., is a severely retarded teenager who has trouble digesting food. He lives solely on Gerber's meat-based formula. The very one that was being discontinued.

I have two sons. What would I do if the substance of their life was to be discontinued? I'd do what Raymond's mother did: I'd call Gerber's, I'd write, I'd pray.

"Don't stop making the food that keeps my son alive!"

All her efforts did no good. Gerber's stood firm.

But someone at Gerber's heard the plea. Someone there understood how Raymond's mother felt. And solved her problem.

Employees at Gerber's acquired the ingredients to make meat-based formula themselves. They volunteered their own time to make and package it.

And the Associated Press ran a story a couple of years ago which opened like this: "Raymond Dunn Jr., turned sixteen years old today, but the profoundly retarded birthday boy feasted not on cake, to which he is allergic, but on the day's greatest gift — the brown, bland formula which keeps him alive."

Understanding how people feel can lead to kindness revolutions.

"Commit yourself to performing one ten-minute act of exceptional customer service per day and to inducing your colleagues to do the same. In a 100-person outfit, that would mean 24,000 new courteous acts per year. Such is the stuff of revolutions."

— *Tom Peters*, A Passion For Excellence

REMEMBER THIS:

You can agree with anyone's feelings without agreeing with the facts.

Each of us is entitled to a point of view, so why bother to change it? Agree with the feelings of the critical person ("I understand how you feel") and solve the problem.

REMEMBER THIS, TOO:

Give people their right to assert themselves without feeling attacked or defensive. When two people reach a point of comfortably expressing their respective opinions (to which all of us have a right), without judgment or defensiveness on either part, good communication will have been born.

HOW TO USE THE RULE OF RESPECT

1. Remember that everyone has the right to feel whatever they wish, and that these feelings might not agree with your feelings.
2. Give credit and support for whatever the other person is feeling with supportive statements such as "I understand how you feel."
3. Continue to support feelings in this manner even when the facts are not correct (from your perspective). You are agreeing with the feelings, not the facts.
4. If a problem exists, go directly to attempting to solve the problem instead of offering reasons as to why the problem occurred.
5. Avoid excessive apologies. Apologize for the inconveniences but not the actions, unless you have intentionally set out to hurt someone, lie, etc.
6. Attempt to find workable compromises when a requested solution cannot be agreed upon.
7. Always follow what you can't do with what you can do in finding solutions.
8. Always give credit to what the other person feels.

Silver Rule

The Rule of Signals:

We Must Be Aware of What
Our Non-Verbal Signals Say

We Must Be Aware of What Our Non-Verbal Signals Say

"Great minds comprehend more in a word, a look, a pressure of the hand than ordinary men in long conversations, or the most eloquent correspondence."

— *Johann Kaspar Lavater*

Your attitude + your signals + your words = your message.

This is the first formula we teach our clients who want to improve their presentation skills.

The "signals" we're referring to here include body language, tone of voice, and eye contact. Poor communicators forget that if these communication factors are not consistent, the message is cloudy.

If a company communicates, "We care about our employees," but their attitudes and signals are not consistent with their words, the message is not clear. And not received.

When a spouse or friend says, "I love you," but their attitudes and signals say otherwise, the message is not clear. And not acknowledged.

Make Sure Your Signals Match Your Words

We communicate more with attitudes and signals than with words.

I have mentioned my son, Wilson, who plays high school football. If you asked me how good a player he was, I might answer, "He's pretty good."

Without hearing my tone, you are unable to get my true meaning from my words alone. My tone speaks louder than my words.

An answer of "Mmmm, he's pretty good . . ." with the words

trailing into silence would be different from, "He's PRETTY good" which would be different still from, "He's pretty GOOD!" The emphasis on different syllables communicates my real feelings.

Watch your tone! It is carrying more of your message than your words alone.

YOUR ATTITUDE + YOUR SIGNALS + YOUR WORDS = YOUR MESSAGE

This is the formula we teach our public speaking classes. It is just as appropriate for one-on-one communication.

We communicate more with our attitudes and our non-verbal signals than we do with our words. When our attitudes and signals don't match our words, the message is garbled.

When we say, "We care about our employees," but don't match those words with our attitudes and signals, the message is unclear.

When we say, "We take care of our customers," but don't match those words with our attitudes and signals, the message is cloudy.

When we say, "I love you," but don't match these words with our attitudes and signals, the message is confusing.

What do your attitudes and signals communicate to those around you?

Match Your Tone to Your Meaning

Most of us are unaware of how our tone sounds to other people. We have heard ourselves so often, and since we know what we are thinking, we forget that our listeners are getting a lot of our message — and our meaning — from the tone of our voice.

I recently had a seminar participant tell me about a particular problem she was having.

"I will sometimes be talking to a co-worker or a friend, and out of the blue they'll ask if I'm angry about something," she began. She then went on to explain that this frequently happened when she wasn't feeling angry in the least.

Obviously her attitudes and her signals were sending some pretty strong messages that overwhelmed her words!

One of the things I suggested was that she record herself on the phone, and in a meeting, or during a conversation (just ask to record the dialogue for notes).

Most people are amazed when they hear their voice — it is so different from what they expected.

In his book, *Developing Skills in Contact Counseling*, Dr. Len Sperry connects these tones with these feelings:

- Monotone voice communicates boredom.
- Slow speed and low pitch communicate depression.
- High voice and emphatic pitch communicate enthusiasm.
- Ascending tone communicates astonishment.
- Abrupt speech communicates defensiveness.
- Terse speed and loud tone communicate anger.
- High pitch and drawn-out speech communicate disbelief.

Defensive, angry, impatient, bored — these are the signals we send by our tone every time we speak. It's worth zeroing in on our tone to set the message straight.

In Communication, Seeing Is Believing

Studies have shown that as much as 80% of what we hear is not retained, but that we do retain as much as 60% of what we see.

And what we see is body language, eye contact, and posture.

By observing these carefully, the listener can ascertain the "real story" being told by the speaker. What they believe is based largely on what they "see" the speaker say.

There are many nuances of body language that could be

addressed, far too many to go into here. But certain techniques can be followed by the communicator to assure that the attitude of choice is conveyed to the listener.

Here are some tips:

To Appear:	Do:
Relaxed	Lean over to one side.
Sincere	Control tendency to "over smile."
Interested	Nod occasionally.
Calm	Control your gestures.
Trusting	Maintain eye contact.
Comforting	Reduce the personal space between you.
Receptive	Lean forward.
Thoughtful	Stroke your chin.
Truthful	Show your palms.

One of my friends, a successful dentist, told me of another dentist who had a practice that had grown so fast he was unable to spend as much time with every patient as he used to. This was noticed by some of his patients, who had commented on his apparent "quicker" treatments.

He began to try something that worked. While not able to spend any more time with each patient, he made it a point to sit in the room with every patient, usually with an empty coffee cup in his hands.

After a few weeks, he began to hear comments about how he was his old self again, always willing to take the time to sit and drink a cup of coffee with his patients.

The impact of his non-verbal communication was recognizable. The message of personal interest and willingness to spend time with his patients was communicated through his visual signals, not through explanations or excuses. Sitting with that coffee cup was much more effective than saying "I wish I could spend more time with you, but my patient load is heavy."

At my seminars, I frequently say that I've never known any-one who got up in the morning, looked in the mirror, and said, "Today I'm going to be a jerk." (This is usually followed by someone shouting out, "Oh yeah, well you haven't met . . . .")

But some people come across as jerks, not so much by what they say — which they are aware of — but rather by the signals they send through their body language and other non-verbal communication.

Imagine a conversation with a "jerk" named Charley.

Charley doesn't look you in the eye. He fidgets around while you are talking. He interrupts you often, and then seems to drift away when you are looking for a response.

Charley slouches in his chair like a cadaver. He doesn't smile. His signals seem to shout, "I don't care."

Do you like talking to Charley?

Charley is a jerk. Or so the people around him think. But he really isn't, he's just sending the wrong signals.

How could Charley communicate non-verbally a little more courteously?

First of all, he needs to understand that he is indeed giving off signals which others are interpreting. He probably doesn't know.

Secondly, he needs to sit up in a posture that is relaxed enough to communicate comfort, but tense enough to com-municate interest. He should incline his body towards the speaker and face him squarely.

Thirdly, he needs to be at eye level, looking the speaker right in the eye.

Finally, he needs to concentrate on listening to the speaker.

By combining these simple, non-verbal signals, Charley can be perceived as interested and sincerely listening. Charley becomes an okay guy.

It has been theorized that each of us has four sides to our behavior. These sides are like window panes, through which people observe us.

It is through these panes that the real us shows.

A technique was developed to help identify our behavior. This technique, the Johari's Window, can be very helpful in closing the gap between how *we* perceive ourselves and how *others* perceive us.

JOHARI'S WINDOW

There are four "windows" to our behavior:
The first window is behavior we are aware of and that we put on display for others.
The second window is behavior that we are aware of but that we control and do not display.
The third window is behavior that we are not aware of and that we don't display. We don't get in touch with it.
The fourth window is behavior that we display but that we're unaware of.
This last window is the danger zone. This is what makes us appear as jerks to others.

Just as it is important to know we are sending messages non-verbally, it is important to be aware of the messages others are sending to us in the same way.

Clichés such as "I had them on the edge of their seats" or "Keep a stiff upper lip" indicate that we have a pretty good natural awareness of some of the language of the body.

By observing the body language of others, we receive their non-verbal signals which we can then compare to their words.

Remember, the message is never clear when the signals and the words don't match.

REMEMBER THIS:

The signals you send through your tone of voice and your body language are more powerful than your words. Make sure they match, and you'll communicate loud and clear.

HOW TO USE THE RULE OF SIGNALS

1. Remember that you are communicating as much non-verbally as you are with your words.

2. Keep your communication as "open" as possible to convey trust. Open palms, arms not crossed, etc.

3. Lean forward to convey interest in what is being said.

4. Beware of speaking "through your fingers." Keep your hands away from your face to convey honesty.

5. Try to communicate at eye level with the person to whom you are speaking.

6. Maintain steady eye contact.

7. Remember that our attitudes and signals communicate more than our words.

Silver Rule

The Rule of Dignity:

We Must Remember That
What We Do Is Not as
Important as How We Do It

We Must Remember That What We Do Is Not as Important as How We Do It

---

"Dignity does not consist of possess-
ing honors, but in deserving them."
                    — Aristotle

In today's society, there are individuals with vastly different economic affluence, from the very poor to the unbelievably rich.

Some people are fortunate enough to have been born into families of wealth, making them the recipients and stewards of fortunes amassed by their parents, grandparents, or even further back. Others achieve personal success and accumulate wealth through their own efforts. Some people have average incomes, while still others are in poverty.

Different breaks, opportunities, education, experience — all of these lead to different career choices and different lifestyles.

Unfortunately, in spite of the many aspects of each individual's life, heritage, interests, and spirit, our typical first question when meeting someone new is "And what do you do?".

What difference does it make?

"My first job was as important as any I ever had. It was my initiation into a man's world. Being a newsboy taught me the meaning of duty. And without a sense of duty, a man is nothing."
                    — Eddie Rickenbacker, World War II Pilot

Treat Every Job With Dignity

Every person's job should be treated the same — with dignity. From the chairman to the mailman, from management to maintenance, jobs are performed better when they are done with dignity.

Our job as communicators is to communicate dignity and respect to everyone we contact — customers, employees, management, family. Everyone.

Does it take more dignity to be a chairman than a mailman? Does it take more dignity to be in management than in maintenance?

Maybe it's time that we treat everyone with the dignity that they deserve as unique individuals, not the dignity that we think their position, or job, or affluence, deserves.

I have a friend. As a young man, he had dreams of a good career, a family, an active life with his wife and children.

The same dreams of all young men.

An interruption in his plans, called World War II, changed a lot of that. A war injury impaired his vision and took away his law career.

So my friend couldn't drive a car.

He couldn't play ball in the back yard with his son, couldn't fish, couldn't practice law.

So my friend sold furniture at a department store for 35 years. And he did his work and raised his family with pride, dignity, respect, and courtesy . . . and never complained.

My friend's name is Bill.

My sons call him Grandpa.

I call him Dad.

He is the nicest man I have ever met.

What we do is not as important as how we do it. And how we do it should be with dignity. That is the measure of our greatness.

I'm reminded of the fellow who asked three stone cutters what they were doing.

The first paused from his work and said, "I'm cutting stone."

The second commented, "I'm making a cornerstone."

The third pondered for a moment and said, "I'm building a cathedral."

Professionalism Is Not a Kind of Job — It's an Attitude

In business communication, people can tell quickly if you have a professional attitude about your job or are just someone working for a paycheck.

Who do you think customers want to deal with? The professionals? The ones more concerned with how they do their jobs than with what they do? Or the amateurs? The ones more concerned with what they (and everyone else) are doing than the way in which they do it?

My point here is simple but important: everyone should be treated with dignity because everyone's job requires dignity. If a job were not important, it probably wouldn't exist.

The people we interact with every day have important jobs. It's time we treated them with the dignity they deserve. If only everyone would do this, all jobs would be performed with dignity, quality, and concern.

And, don't forget, your job is important, too. Do it with pride!

I once had a friend named Andy. Andy was a welder, a darned good one and proud of it.

Andy had a foreman in Memphis who used to say Andy was the best welder he had ever seen . . . that Andy's work had its own identity.

The foreman moved to Minnesota to head up a construction job. Months later, a welder wanted to take the required welding test to work on the job.

As soon as the foreman saw the test weld, he cried out, "Hire this man immediately! The only man I've ever seen who could weld like this is Andy Anderson in Memphis!"

It turned out the test weld was Andy Anderson's, who had come all the way to Minnesota to apply for a job with the foreman who treated him with dignity and respect.

How he did the job was important to Andy. And he was willing to go all the way to Minnesota to work with a foreman who felt the same way.

How we do a job should be what's important to us, too — much more important than what job it is we do.

Booker T. Washington once said, "When we can teach our children that it takes as much dignity to plow a field as it does to write a poem, we will achieve socially."

Communicate this in everything you work at: "I'm proud of what I do. Let me show you how this job is done well."

Every time you reach out to take your paycheck, you are stating that you have done the best you can for that pay. If you are giving less than your best, you are cheating the company. Don't be upset, then, when the company cheats you!

Likewise, it is just as important to let others know when we notice how they do their jobs. Their dignity shows, for instance, when they do just that little bit more that separates their work from all others.

There is a simple way to let others know you appreciate the work they do. It may be the cleaning person at your office, it might be the mailman, or your secretary, or your boss.

It is easy to remember, simple, but amazingly powerful.

It goes like this . . .

"Thank you."

REMEMBER THIS:

Every job is important. It deserves respect. And it deserves to be done with dignity and pride.

It is not the job, but the doing that is the true measure of success.

And if doing the job well is the measurement of success, dignity is the measure of greatness.

HOW TO USE THE RULE OF DIGNITY

1. Remember that what we do is more important than how we do it.

2. Perform each daily task as if it were important.

3. Ask yourself "If I worked for me, would I be pleased? Would I be willing to pay more to keep me happy?"

4. Treat everyone with whom you have contact as if their job is important, regardless of the monetary value or cultural status put on the job.

5. Watch the people around you specifically to catch them doing something right.

6. Thank people when you spot them doing something right.

Silver Rule

The Rule of Support:
We Must Look for the Greatness
in Ourselves and Others

We Must Look for the Greatness in Ourselves and Others

"When I was research head of General Motors and wanted a problem solved, I'd place a table outside the meeting room with a sign: 'Leave slide rules here.' If I didn't do that, I'd find some engineer reaching for his slide rule. Then he'd be on his feet saying, 'Boss, you can't do it.'"
— *Charles F. Kettering*

Isn't it wonderful to be around those people who are so perfect themselves that they can't find anything good about anybody else? Always putting down the other guy, both to his face and behind his back? The type who can always find a reason why your idea is going to fail?

They're the same type that Thomas Edison, the Wright Brothers, Gallileo, Benjamin Franklin, and others subtly told to shut up. (My favorite Chinese expression is, "Man who believe something impossible should not interrupt Man doing it.")

PORPOISES Love to Dream

The following conversation is said to have occurred at one of the nation's largest utility companies:

The Boss (LION, the leader) said, "We must discover a way to harness other natural energy sources to eliminate nuclear energy."

The Marketing Director (PORPOISE, the visionary) suggested, "Why don't we build a pipeline from the earth to the sun and capture the energy of the sun for use here on earth?"

The Department Manager (KOALA, the team player) added, "We'll need architects, engineers, builders, and supplies."

The Accountant (FOX, the cautious thinker) asked, "What will we do when the pipeline gets near the sun and the heat prevents our workers from going further?"

To which the Marketing Director replied, "No problem. We'll do the work at night!"

While the PORPOISE in this example may have gone a little over the top in his dreaming, many of us can relate to times when our dreams were destroyed by someone telling us, "You can't do that."

Sometimes this is good. And it is a natural tendency for some behavioral styles to pepper others with logic and reasoning (pay close attention here, LIONS and FOXES). But there are many times when tiny dreams can become big realities.

Roger Bannister was told he'd never walk again after an accident injured his legs. And he ran the first four-minute mile.

John Kennedy was too young to be president, Jack Nicklaus was too old to win the Masters. Doug Flutie was too short to be a college quarterback. Mugsy Bogues was too short to play pro basketball.

All were surrounded by friends and relatives who told them, "You can't do that."

Are you a dream builder or dream buster? Do you encourage going the distance or quitting before you finish? Do you look for the good in everyone you meet, no matter what?

A good communicator looks for that "good light" in everyone, even when it is barely a flicker. The other person knows when you're looking for it, and feels a kinship with you.

Build Your Own Dreams, Too

Over the years, I've practiced a method which has helped me focus on my dreams and determine which ones I can turn into reality.

The process is called visualization, and it is powerful when practiced.

Every source from scripture to psychiatry shows examples of how people can achieve great things if they can actually picture themselves succeeding in their efforts.

Whether it's athletics, sales, fiscal goals, or personal achievement, when we clearly see ourselves reaching our goals, we come closer to making them real.

The same is true when we picture ourselves failing. How often have you golfers had a shot for the green with a water hazard between you and your goal? And you said to yourself, "Don't hit it in the water." Which, of course, is exactly where the ball landed.

And then there's the second serve in tennis. On a crucial point. "Don't hit it in the net," you think. OOPS.

Simply put, we each carry a picture of ourselves in our mind. It is as clear as the pictures we carry of our loved ones in our wallets. Unfortunately, it's frequently the wrong kind of picture.

We cannot consistently perform in a manner contrary to the picture we have of ourselves. We can fool it temporarily, but we can't keep it up. If our picture is of an unhappy, or overweight, or unsuccessful person, that is what we will be.

The good news is that we can change the picture. And once the picture is changed, we become that person.

Change the picture to a non-smoker and we become one. Change the picture to a thinner person and we become one. Change the picture to a confident, peak performer and that is what we become.

Now, this doesn't eliminate the need for diets, practice, or any other support mechanism for improvement. It simply assures us that they will work, for by changing the mental picture, in our mind we have already achieved the goal. Now, all we are doing is "acting it out." We already know the ending.

It doesn't fail.

Change Your Self-Picture

How do we change our pictures of ourselves?

We begin by setting a specific goal. Maybe to quit smoking. Or perhaps to lose 40 pounds. Or to make the Million Dollar Sales Club. Or to shoot a 6 handicap in golf. It could be anything. Just make it specific.

Let me state here the importance of being specific in describing your goals. They must be measurable. For example, your goal might be to improve a particular athletic endeavor, such as golf. In this example, a poor goal statement would read, "I want to be a better golfer." This objective is not specific enough to recognize when it has been reached; therefore, it is impossible to imagine. When does one become a "better golfer?" Or thinner? Or smoking less? Or a better sales person?

State the goal in a specific, measurable manner, such as "I want to be a 2 handicap" "I want to sell a million in sales," etc.

This accomplishes two goals. First of all, it lets the visualizer know when the goal has been met. But more importantly, it allows for the development of a clear mental image of how the performer will look and feel when the specific goal has been achieved.

Then make a list of all the reasons this goal can't be reached. Remember, this is a list of the reasons we can't do something, not the reasons we won't do something.

For example, suppose my goal is to become a lawyer. But I choose not to give up my work or leisure time to go to law school. It's not that I can't do this. I simply won't. I choose not to make the sacrifice. It's my choice, but it's not a reason why I CAN'T become a lawyer.

Or I may choose not to write a novel because I don't want to invest the time or risk the rejection. But these aren't the reasons I can't do it.

This is where we separate fantasy from reality.

A lot of what we (and our well-meaning advisors) see as logical reasons a goal can't be reached is really based on our decisions not to make the sacrifices necessary to reach our goal. They're not "can'ts" but "won'ts."

Get the point? As you list the reasons you can't achieve your specific goal, you will probably be in for a surprise.

The list will probably be blank.

About the time I think of age as being a legitimate "can't," I think of an aging Sir Winston Churchill becoming a world leader late in his life. Or I think of George Foreman becoming the heavyweight champ at the unheard-of-age of 45.

So look at the reasons you can't achieve your goal. And relish the fact that there are none!

Then, make a list of all the ways you will look, feel, and act when you have achieved your goal.

Describe the clothes you will wear when you are thinner. Describe the feel, look, and smell of the new car you will drive when you achieve your sales goal. Go into great detail so you can better picture yourself achieving your goal.

Finally, list brief, present-tense affirmations that reinforce the achievement of your goal. Not "I will" or "I can" statements, but "I am" statements.

"I weigh 160 pounds" "I am a 6 handicap golfer" "I am a million dollar producer."

Then go into action.

Get the Picture — and Succeed

Twice a day, relax briefly by taking three deep breaths and exhaling. Relax your entire body.

Once you're in a relaxed state of mind, picture yourself as you would be achieving your goal. Watch every detail. Notice how you walk, talk, carry yourself.

Picture yourself performing in the manner you plan to achieve from every perspective. See how the world looks from your eyes. See how you fit into your surroundings. See how others react to you. Refine, enhance, and perfect your performance as you proceed.

Try to experience all of the senses of your picture. The smell of the gym, the feeling of your new clothes, the sound of recognition at the annual meeting, whatever. Experience them as if you were right in the picture.

The more vivid the picture, the more the mind will accept it as real.

If you have trouble picturing yourself in a successful endeavor, model the way you act in your picture after someone who has already achieved your goal. Notice their every movement . . . their confidence, their swagger and pace, their calmness. Then picture yourself in that same manner.

If specific performance is desired, such as athletics or even public speaking, view yourself performing the event initially as you would view a movie, as if on a screen and you're looking at yourself from the outside. After the event has been performed successfully, "move" within your own body and experience the successful performance in your mind.

As you mentally rehearse, you will begin to crystallize that performance in your mind. You will begin to find that you can recall these peak performances in your mind, time and time again. You will be able to see the picture of yourself as successfully achieving your goals.

And as you do, guess what will happen: your body will follow.

Just as your body is following the picture you have in your mind right now, it will adjust itself to your new picture.

And you will become that picture.

And you will have discovered the greatness that was hidden in you.

    Legend tells us of a man who watched the Wright Brothers work on their flying device. "It'll never work," he said.
    He watched as they carefully drug it to a point at Kitty Hawke. "It'll never work," he repeated.
    He watched as Orville Wright boarded the craft. "It'll never work," he shouted after him.
    And he watched as the plane ascended. And flew.
    "Well, if you're going to do it THAT way . . . "

There Is Something Great in Everyone

In Florence, Italy, there is a statue. It is called "David." It is one of the most powerful, moving works of art ever created by man.

And there is a beautiful story associated with this statue.

It seems that the people of Florence commissioned a great artist for this project. When he arrived in Florence, he inspected the large block of marble he was to work with and declared it unfit, not perfect enough. He refused to do the work.

The people of Florence were mortified and didn't know

what to do. So they contacted another artist of the day, a fellow named Michelangelo.

They said, "Mike, can you work on this for us?" And he said, "Sure can." And he created this living, breathing statue of David.

When the townspeople first saw this masterpiece, they asked Michelangelo how he could create this work when the other sculptor said he couldn't.

And Michelangelo said, "The greatness was in there all the time. I just had to look for it and cut away all the stuff that didn't belong."

It was there all the time.

People respond differently to others who look for the good in them. They try harder, they give more, they respond better. Sometimes they even achieve greatness.

Like Bob Wieland.

Bob Wieland is a runner. Like me. Bob Wieland is a slow runner, also like me.

And, like me, Bob Wieland once decided to run in a marathon.

The difference is, I quit. And Bob Wieland set the record for the worst time in the New York Marathon in 1984. He finished in four days.

I could have run 26.2 miles in four days. In four days, I could have done that. And when I think about Bob Wieland, I wish I hadn't quit.

Because ANYBODY can run a marathon in four days.

Did I tell you that Bob Wieland doesn't have any legs? They were blown off during an explosion in Vietnam.

He doesn't use a bicycle or platform with wheels to run. He pulls himself along with his arms, using padded gloves to protect his hands. He pulled himself for four days and 26.2 miles.

Through the rain.

Through the dark.

People honked at him. Dogs barked at him.

The sponsors of the marathon heard about this man who was still in the race after four days. And they came and cheered him on as he crossed the finish line.

Someone asked him how it felt to finish last. "Last?" he said, "I finished ahead of the 1,500 people who quit!"

The world saw the greatness in Bob Wieland that day.

Let People Know When You See Their Greatness

There's greatness in you, and me, and everyone you meet.

Their greatness may be in the form of kindness, beauty, humor, wisdom . . . their dignity. Not necessarily great acts or accumulated wealth. When we see that greatness, let the other person know it!

TALK ABOUT THE GREATNESS YOU SEE
Go home tonight and tell a child, any child, that there is greatness in them.
Affirm these children every day.
And then treat your employees like they were children, too.

One of the most meaningful moments of my life occurred two years ago when I took my oldest son, Ted, to college.

My sons have been my best friends and now one of those friends was embarking on a new life. It was one of those magnificent moments in a father's life, a time when the dreams of a child become clearly etched on the face of a young man.

I wanted to pay Ted the highest tribute that I could. Seeing the greatness in him, his warmth, his sense of humor, his values, I told him that most parents have sons who want to be like the Dad.

In my case, I am a Dad who wants to be like his sons.

A recent study at an Ivy League school indicated that 90% of all teaching was centered around "how-to" knowledge and 10% dealt with attitudes. And that 10% was usually found in extracurricular activities like band, dramatics, athletics, and so forth.

Another study asked businessmen to rate the importance of an employee's "how-to" skills, as opposed to the attitude of the employee. Attitude received a 90% rating in importance, "how-to" skills came in at 10%.

Is something amiss here?

Maybe it's time that we let others know that we see what is inside them. That we see, and celebrate, the capacity for greatness inside.

Look for that greatness and other people will want to be around you. Because you recognize, and value, what is best in them.

The finest compliment that anyone can give is this: "I feel better about myself when I am with you."

REMEMBER THIS:

Visualize greatness for yourself, and you can begin to achieve it. Make a point to look for that greatness, and you will see the respect that you give — and get — begin to grow and grow.

HOW TO USE THE RULE OF SUPPORT

1. Remember that everyone has a dream.

2. Be supportive of the other person's dreams and visions.

3. Establish high goals and dreams for yourself.

4. Clearly picture how you will look, think, feel, and act when you have achieved your goals.

5. Affirm your success with short, present tense, positive statements.

6. Affirm your success often during the day.

7. Relax and visualize your success at least twice a day.

8. Eliminate any negative thoughts and doubts the moment they come to mind.

Communication on the Job

Communication on the Job

"Man does not live by GNP alone."
— Paul A. Samuelson

Each of the rules we have discussed apply just as effectively whether you're attempting to engage in positive communication at home, in groups, or in business. By utilizing a little thoughtfulness, we can become more effective communicators in any of these environments.

On the job, however, there are a few additional pointers which might improve relationships at work. These deal with the specific use of credit, thanks, and praise.

A sure way to communicate well with anyone is to give proper credit to the other person. An idea, a solution to a problem, a great meal, a good conversation, anything!

Unfortunately, especially in business communication, the competition for recognition is so fierce that most individuals want to grab all the glory they can for themselves. In addition to being self-destructive, it does nothing to foster good relations with other people.

Give the Credit Away

The concept is quite simple: when credit is due someone else, give it to them.

When the actual credit is shared, give it to the other person! Again and again, give the credit to someone else.

When you give the credit away, two things happen.

First of all, the proper credit ALWAYS comes home. Doesn't make any difference who claims it, it always becomes obvious who should get the credit.

So what difference does giving it away make?

By giving the credit away, other people are drawn to share with you . . . and willing to ask you to aid in the development of ideas and strategies because they know you won't be grabbing all the glory. This will expose you to many more opportunities and new ideas than before!

Show Your Approval

There are two wonderful phrases to incorporate into your regular vocabulary. Phrases to use soon and often:

1. "You did well."
2. "You'll do well."

It makes no difference how you package these phrases; the words you actually use are not important. The important thing is to let the other person know you recognize their good work and that you have confidence in their ability.

In business today, there are many trite rules and phrases which fall under the category of "overused."

I dare you to overuse these phrases!

I also challenge you to "make a difference" in your firm or organization by stepping up and doling out credit.

I recently spent time on the Board of a company where the Chairman had an interesting habit of referring to the company as "my company" when things were good. However, the minute things turned sour, the "my" would turn into "they" (as in the management). In other words, credit was claimed for the good, rejected for the bad. How motivated was management to do well when the credit always went to one person?

Unfortunately, this is too often the case. Individuals who strive to take the credit and reject the responsibility for errors seem to be par for the course.

One of the most frequent complaints that is heard, both in business and at home, is "I'm just not appreciated."

How hard is it to stop for a moment and praise someone?

How much trouble would it be just to say a few words when we catch someone doing something right?

But many people rarely, and some never, seem to get around to praising other people.

Here are some tips to help you spread the praise:

PRAISE SINCERELY.

We have all been around people who lavish praise and compliments on others to the extent that it becomes obvious that their intention is to either get praise back or become liked themselves.

We should give our praise sincerely so that it is appreciated, but not hold it back.

Husband look good today? Tell him. Don't assume "He knows I think he looks good." He wants to hear it!

Child do something right at school? Tell her! You can't overdo it here.

Notice an employee's hairdo, new suit, good job? If you like it or notice it, tell them.

PRAISE OFTEN.

If Your Praise Is Sincere, Use It Often

You will find a difference in the way people behave around you if you praise and compliment them.

I used to work with a very good manager, but he had one severe problem when it came to his employees — he wouldn't compliment them. Occasionally, when he would counsel them, they would explain to him that they would be more effective if he would occasionally compliment their work.

"I'm just not very good at that type of stuff," was his reply. Nonsense.

It doesn't take anything more than thought and effort to compliment someone.

Remember, What Goes Around Comes Around

Here are a couple more simple communication rules for business:

- The way you treat your employees is the way they will treat your customers.
- The way you communicate with your employees today is the way they will communicate with their employees tomorrow.

If you think this puts a lot of responsibility on you, the supervisor, you are exactly right.

This is where many companies fail at endeavors to improve "corporate communication." They talk the talk, but they don't walk the walk.

And that doesn't go very far.

REMEMBER THIS:

Whenever you give away the praise, it will come right back to you. And then more than one person will be happy.

Communicating to Groups

Communicating to Groups

"There are few wild beasts more to be dreaded than a talking man having nothing to say."
— *Jonathan Swift*

One of the most important skills that a business person should develop is that of speaking before groups.

Some people have a natural knack for public speaking. Others dread it fearfully. Virtually all surveys of "greatest fears" place public speaking at or near the top of the list.

Remembering a few key points can help us become world-class speakers in presentations before groups of people, whether it's a group of three or three thousand. And while this topic deserves a book of its own, I will cover some of the most important points to remember.

If We Don't Know It, We Won't Discuss It

Or, in other words, if we don't know our material we won't talk about it.

For many speakers, this is scary. Taking the podium without our prompts . . . those written-out speeches, index cards, and other aids.

We should command enough knowledge of our material so that we don't need to read a speech. Over-reliance on notes is a major distraction to an audience; every time we look down at our notes, we lose some of our audience.

It is better to know our material and use a manner which is more conversational when speaking to our audience. They are forgiving when we pause to remember something, but less forgiving when we stumble along.

I recently had a client, the CEO of a major firm, who was preparing for a presentation to his shareholders. He practiced his presentation for me. Reading it. It didn't sound like his normal, sincere, person-to-person way of speaking. It sounded just like what it was — something that was prepared and then read.

When he finished, I asked him why he didn't just let one of his VP's read the speech.

"Because they want to hear me," he replied.

"But that's not you."

And it wasn't. He was warm, sincere, and relaxed when he spoke naturally. When he read, he was stilted and cold. It wasn't him.

And it's not any of us when we read a prepared speech.

A preferred way to use notes is to have brief one-word or two-word descriptors written on 3" x 5" cards to lead you along during your presentation.

But there are a couple of times when it is okay to read.

One is when you are quoting directly from someone else. The other is when you are quoting figures of some kind. In both of these cases it is appropriate, possibly even desirable, to read directly from the sources.

Break Your Presentation Into Small Pieces

World-class presentations are actually a number of small presentations pieced together. At the Center for Spoken Communication we call this "file formatting." We piece small files together, built around our 3" x 5" cards, to create our message.

This accomplishes a lot of things.

First of all, it gives our listeners an opportunity to tune us back in after they have tuned us out. And believe me, they *will* tune us out.

I don't care if it's Billy Graham, Norman Vincent Peale, or

Paul Harvey, listeners do not concentrate on every word that is said. Their minds are capable of processing much more data than that.

Accepting that premise, why not make it easy to rejoin the presentation as it proceeds? We do that by creating short message segments of one to three minutes and then transitioning them with a statement or statements to support our main theme.

For example, my presentation may consist of six or seven of these files, each containing a story, or point, or information which supports my main theme. By mentioning the main theme following each of these files, my listener can leave remembering only three or four files, but still get the big picture.

Compare that to a long speech which hits at the theme at the beginning and end alone, by which time a number of listeners have drifted off to la-la land.

Think of a speech as an album or CD of your favorite music. These usually contain a dozen or so songs, each of which is different. When a song comes on that sounds particularly good to you, you tune in a little stronger. When one comes on that doesn't appeal to you as much, you tend to tune it out a little.

And even when an album has a very special, favorite song, you don't want to listen to just that song for an hour.

Effective presentations are the same way. They contain variety through these "files," some of which are more appealing to different people than others. And, if we are aware of what our audience wants, we can make sure that we give them something that appeals to all their different styles.

Here are examples of what different audience styles like to hear:

LIONS like to have bottom line, summary presentations. To appeal to them, our presentation files should include bullet points, like "three ways to . . . " "six points for . . . ," etc. They are selective listeners and will not listen to everything that is said. To please them, be concise.

PORPOISES like stimulating, upbeat presentations. For them, our files should have personal stories and humor. They like to laugh and be entertained. To please them, be energetic.

KOALAS like sincere presentations. Include files which contain an honest evaluation of why this presentation is important. To please them, be warm and helpful.

FOXES like informative presentations. Their files would be loaded with data. To please them, offer plenty of facts, figures, and time to process what is said.

By remembering that any group consists of different styles, we can "feed" them a little of the food that they like in our presentations instead of feeding them all the same food, which will only satisfy a small portion of listeners.

We Must Use Humor and Personal Stories

World-class presentations involve the use of humor and personal stories. PORPOISES and KOALAS demand this.

However, most speakers tend to stay on their information. We call this their safety zone. It is a tendency to discuss the information we are most comfortable with, being a little hesitant to venture off into humor and stories of a personal nature.

This is a big mistake. Your audience wants to hear about you. This is the only way they can grow to relate to you. Only by knowing a little about your beliefs, background, and feelings can they come to relate to you. And this relating is what effective presentations are all about.

I don't mean to imply that we must go into a lot of detail about our personal lives. What I do mean is we need to make brief, occasional references to what it is that makes us tick so our audiences can learn a little about us.

"As I was taking my son to college for the first time . . ." "When my daughter and I returned from her music lesson, I heard on the radio . . ." "As a tried and true Cardinals fan . . . ."

All of these types of statements tell a little about us and create relating opportunities with our audiences.

Humor works the same way. However, ineffective humor can kill a presentation or speech. There are two times to use humor. And only two.

We can use humor when we KNOW we are going to be funny. Nothing is better than getting a big laugh from our group. Nothing is worse that trying to be funny and failing. If you are sure that your humor will work, use it.

And we can also use humor when we know we can recover from not being funny.

There is a simple way to accomplish this.

Remember, we are not trying to be comedians, we are trying to get our message across. By making sure that our personal stories and humor support the main message, we can recover from not being funny with a quick transition that says, "The reason that I tell that story is . . . ."

Say this calmly and quickly and the audience is no longer concerned with the humor of the story, but with the message. In effect we are saying, "I'm telling you this not to be funny as much as to support my theme. If you find it humorous, that's great. But its primary purpose is to support my major message."

The best humor is self-deprecating humor. It is always okay to poke fun at ourselves — our size, our age, our habits — anything that allows us to laugh at ourselves aids in building relationships with a group.

We Must Have a Reason for Speaking to Our Group

How many times have you listened to a speaker and wondered why you were even being asked to listen?

Normally, this occurs when a speaker feels they are eloquent enough to get by without any message or point to make, or when a speaker is not properly matched to the audience (imagine a presentation on retirement at a high school).

We can give our message a four-point review to make sure that it is appropriate for our group. It is the same review we suggested using in our chapter on Listening on page 48. By answering these questions, we can be comfortably assured that we have a reason for speaking to the audience.

What is my message? What is the central theme I want to talk about? Many speakers get up to talk without having a basic message to convey.

What is the basis of my message? It might be observations, experiences, something we've read. Whatever it is, we need to let our audience know there is something that makes us qualified to discuss this.

Why is it important to my audience? If we can answer this one, we have it made. If we think it is important to our audience, and we let them know it is important for them to hear it, they will be forgiving of many speaking flaws and usually interested. Even when they don't agree with our point of view. However, if we can't come up with a reason it is important for them to hear our message, it shouldn't be presented.

What action do I want my audience to take? This can be something we encourage them to do, an attitude we want to develop, some new developments they should be on the alert for. In every case, there should be a specific action we challenge them to take.

If we can answer these four questions, we have sufficient reason to ask our audience to invest their time in listening to us speak. If we can't answer these questions, we shouldn't be making our presentation.

Speak as You Would to an Individual

Speaking to groups is no different from speaking to an individual. Yet many of us drastically change our tone and demeanor when speaking to groups of people.

One good exercise I have found to help speakers who don't use a natural style of speaking is to role play. I ask them how they would address a group of high school seniors they were responsible for during a class trip to Florida.

They would be passionate in their belief in the importance of following rules. They would be firm in their delivery. They would be sincere in their concern. They would be detailed in their direction.

Their attitude would convey much more than their words. And their message would be clear.

That is the way to speak to a group. With a message in which you believe, a passion in your belief that it is important, and a natural style that lets your attitude shine through.

From a mute Helen Keller to a dynamic Jesse Jackson, the passion and attitudes of our messages are the lights that our audiences see and remember.

EPILOGUE

I have written this book in the same style I use when I teach my platform presentation clients to speak.

It is written in an attempt to appeal to the different styles of readers: LIONS, PORPOISES, KOALAS, and FOXES.

For the LIONS, I have included chapter summaries and "how-to's" so that you can go directly to the bottom-line to find out what is included and how to use it.

For the PORPOISES, I have included personal anecdotes, quotations, and inspirational stories to help you remember the message of the book.

For you KOALAS, I hope the sincerity of my message aids you in recalling the key points of the book.

And for you FOXES, I have attempted to provide enough data so that you may follow the steps for better communication.

Incidentally, for those of you who may be wondering, I am a PORPOISE.

And, as such, I am inclined to leave you with a thought. It is a poem which I can remember, but I am at a loss to identify the author or source (PORPOISES are bad about details and organization). It goes like this:

God said, "Build a better world." And I said, "How?
The world is so big and complicated now
And I'm so young and helpless
What is it I can do?"
And God in all His wisdom said,
"Just build a better you."

Here's to a better you.

Skill-Building Resources

Guide to Anticipated Behavior

Research into behavior and communication has indicated there are four dominant communication styles. These styles describe the way individuals tend to communicate and behave in specific circumstances.

Instructions: Look at each row of adjectives across the page. Determine which word best describes you as you see yourself (not as you would like to be seen or think you are seen by others). Place a "4" next to this word. Then place a "3" beside the next most descriptive word, a "2" beside one of the remaining words which describes you, and a "1" next to the final word, which is the one you feel least describes you.

Example: _4_ Powerful _1_ Influential _2_ Stable _3_ Calculating

There should be no ties. Be as honest and brief in deciding as you can. Your first choice is usually your most accurate.

Remember this: there are no right or wrong answers, no best styles. We need all types in our world, our lives, and our work. Celebrate the difference!

Column A	Column B	Column C	Column D
___ Powerful	___ Influential	___ Stable	___ Calculating
___ Fearless	___ Upbeat	___ Methodical	___ Hesitant
___ Confident	___ Effervescent	___ Calm	___ Rational
___ Heroic	___ Welcoming	___ Steadying	___ Analytical
___ Impatient	___ Spontaneous	___ Protective	___ Accurate
___ Determined	___ Excitable	___ Agreeable	___ Skeptical
___ Dominant	___ Convincing	___ Unassuming	___ Inquisitive
___ Competitive	___ Verbose	___ Faithful	___ Clever
___ Explorative	___ Social	___ Laid-back	___ Particular
___ Vigorous	___ Personable	___ Peaceful	___ Constant
___ TOTAL	___ TOTAL	___ TOTAL	___ TOTAL

Add up the numbers in each vertical column. Total points per "animal" will display your general behavioral tendencies. The higher the total, the stronger the tendency.

COLUMN A	COLUMN B	COLUMN C	COLUMN D
LIONS_____	PORPOISES_____	KOALAS_____	FOXES_____

How to Understand the Animals Better

If we understand the typical behaviors of our "animals," we'll learn more about how to interact and communicate with them effectively. Use this chart as a guide for signals and symptoms that these "animals" generally display.

	Usually Want	Are Irritated By	Under Stress Will	All Animals Like Praise
LIONS	• To be in control • To feel important • To downplay their feelings • To implement changes • To say what's on their minds	• Inefficiency • Indecisiveness • Overthinking	• Cause conflict • Fight verbally or physically • Use short, terse communication	• Want praise for their **RESULTS** • Praise them by saying, "Good job. Thanks to you, we got the order."
PORPOISES	• To interact with people • To function with few details • To enjoy excitement • To be included • To get feedback	• Mundane routines • Overly complex details • Lack of stimulating activity • Challenges to their "methods"	• Leave the stressful situation • Change the subject • Ignore the stressful source • Communicate by rambling unclear sentences	• Want praise for **HOW** they did the work, not the results • Praise them by saying, "Great work. I noticed your efforts from the beginning."
KOALAS	• To have order • To work as part of a team • To establish long-term relationships • To perform repetitive tasks • To be valued	• Impatience • Insensitivity • Numerous changes • Persistent inquiries about the "status quo" or time schedules	• Tolerate stress well but may be overly quiet • Internalize feelings • Communicate non-verbally; withholds true feelings and comments	• Want praise for their efforts and **PERSISTENCE** • Praise them by saying, "Good work. I appreciate your hanging in there on this."
FOXES	• To know how something works • To be right • To avoid surprises • To avoid aggression • To avoid criticism • To function in an organized environment	• Disorganization • Inaccuracy • Aggressiveness • Forced "impulse" decisions • Criticism of performance	• Try to avoid stress • Withdraw, plan next move • Communicate with nit-picking or critical conversation	• Want praise for their **ACCURACY** • Praise them by saying, "Very nicely done. Your work was excellent and complete."

A Checklist of Communication Skills: Self-Evaluation

The following checklist can help you measure how well you communicate. While this form is intended for self-evaluation, the next page in this book can be used to get another person's evaluation (or several) of how well you communicate.

Just put a check in the column that best describes you for each of the communication skills. Be honest with yourself!

Always	Sometimes	Never	
____	____	____	Do I act as if I appreciate our differences?
____	____	____	Do I listen?
____	____	____	Am I non-defensive when criticized or questioned?
____	____	____	Do I act as if I understand your situation?
____	____	____	Do I use your name and look you in the eye?
____	____	____	Do I show respect for how you do your job?
____	____	____	Do I give you time to talk?
____	____	____	Do I encourage your dreams and visions?
____	____	____	Do I communicate interest and respect through my body language?
____	____	____	Do I act as if I have respect for your point of view?

If you answered Always for most of these questions, you're well on your way towards communicating with thoughtfulness and kindness. And you know which skills you need to improve to get there!

If most of your checks are in the Sometimes column, you probably need to do some work on communicating respectfully with others.

If most of your checks were under Never, you are probably reading this book alone right now because no one wants to be around you.

A Checklist of Communication Skills: A Listener's Evaluation

Please evaluate this person's communication skills by checking the column that best describes them. Be honest! This person is depending on your help.

Always Sometimes Never

____ ___ ___   Does this person act as if he/she appreciates our differences?

____ ___ ___   Does this person listen?

____ ___ ___   Is this person non-defensive when criticized or questioned?

____ ___ ___   Does this person show understanding for my situation?

____ ___ ___   Does this person use my name and look me in the eye?

____ ___ ___   Does this person show respect for how I do my job?

____ ___ ___   Does this person give me time to talk?

____ ___ ___   Does this person encourage my dreams and visions?

____ ___ ___   Does this person communicate interest and respect through his/her body language?

____ ___ ___   Does this person show respect for my point of view?

If you answered Always for most of these questions, take the time to let the other person know how much you appreciate their courteous communication.

If you answered Sometimes for most of these questions, let the other person know how they might improve on their communication with you. ("I appreciate our communication when you . . . . ")

If you answered Never to most of these questions, don't bother to discuss it . . . they aren't listening anyway. Convey your message concisely and quickly. Demonstrate your interest in communicating clearly with them — maybe it will be contagious.

Group Presentation Checklist

Use this checklist to evaluate how well you communicate in a small or large group. This form can also be given to others to help you measure your group presentation skills. Check the column that best describes your normal presentation skills.

Always Sometimes Never

Always	Sometimes	Never	
____	____	____	Was my message clear?
____	____	____	Did I have a basis for my message?
____	____	____	Was it important for my audience?
____	____	____	Did I have action for them to take?
____	____	____	Did I appeal to the different communication styles in my audience?
____	____	____	Did I make it clear how long I would talk?
____	____	____	Did I avoid using any unnecessary or distracting movements or mannerisms?
____	____	____	Did I make eye contact with the audience as if I were speaking to them as individuals?
____	____	____	Did I use brief, concise prompts instead of a written speech?
____	____	____	Did I get out of my "safety zone" and use personal stories and humor to support my message?

If you answered Always to most of these questions, you don't need to be told that you are effective as a speaker . . . the standing ovations you are getting already affirm that.

If you answered Sometimes to most of these questions, you can move to World-Class speaking with some practice and training.

If you answered Never to most of these questions, it might be nice to wake up your audience after your next presentation. Or, consider videotaping your next presentation and review your skills based on this checklist.

RESOURCES AND SUGGESTED READING

Manuel J. Smith, *When I Say No, I Feel Guilty.* New York: Bantam Books, 1975.

Tony Alessandra and Michael J. O'Connor, *People Smart.* La Jolla: Keynote Publishing Co., 1992.

Randy Pennington and Marc Bockmon, *On My Honor, I Will.* New York: Warner Books, Inc., 1992.

Ron Hoff, *I Can See You Naked.* Kansas City: Andrews and McMeel, 1992.

Robert Bolton, *People Skills.* New York: Simon & Schuster, Inc., 1979.

Brian Tracy, *Maximum Achievement.* New York: Simon & Schuster, Inc., 1993.

Dr. Len Sperry, *Developing Skills in Contact Counseling.* Massachusetts: Addison-Wesley, 1975.